Prayer Can Move Your Mountains

Not For the Faint of Heart

Charles F. Keim

WestBow
PRESS
A DIVISION OF THOMAS NELSON

WestBow Press books may be ordered through booksellers or by contacting:

WestBow Press
A Division of Thomas Nelson
1663 Liberty Drive
Bloomington, IN 47403
www.westbowpress.com
1-(866) 928-1240

Because of the dynamic nature of the Internet, any Web addresses or links contained in this book may have changed since publication and may no longer be valid. The views expressed in this work are solely those of the author and do not necessarily reflect the views of the publisher, and the publisher hereby disclaims any responsibility for them.

Any people depicted in stock imagery provided by Thinkstock are models, and such images are being used for illustrative purposes only.

Certain stock imagery © Thinkstock.

ISBN: 978-1-4497-0696-8 (sc)
ISBN: 978-1-4497-0697-5 (dj)
ISBN: 978-1-4497-0695-1 (e)

Library of Congress Control Number: 2010939607

Printed in the United States of America

WestBow Press rev. date: 11/24/2010

Prayer Can Move Your Mountains:
Not for the Faint of Heart

Matthew 17:20b
"For I assure you: If you have faith the size of a mustard seed,
you will tell this mountain, 'Move from here to there,' and it
will move. Nothing will be impossible for you."

By Charles Keim

Bible Abbreviation Key

KJV	King James Version
NKJV	New King James Version
CSV	Christian Standard Version
Amp	Amplified Bible

CONTENTS

PROLOGUE

In 2000, a little book written by Bruce Wilkinson called *The Prayer of Jabez* made the bestsellers list. It was an instant success for the hope that it brought to millions of people. Many read, claimed the prayer for themselves, and as so often is the case, abused and misused the prayer for selfish gain. For many, no consideration was given to the will of God. No limit was placed on the appeal of enlarging one's borders, one's health, or one's wealth. Consequently, many were left disillusioned and frustrated with another get-rich-quick claim with God as their pawn. They failed to understand the responsibility that comes with the Lord enlarging one's territory.

They also failed to understand that God sometimes answers with a resounding *no*. Not everything we want is good for us, and God, for our own sake, sometimes withholds what we ask. James 4:3 tells us, "You ask and you receive not, because you ask amiss, that you may consume it upon your lusts." There is a spiritual principal here that warns us to keep our wants in check. God is faithful to give us His will for our lives and He will give us what we ask when we ask according to His will. Jesus Himself demonstrated this principle when He prayed to the Father, "not My will but Thine be done." God is not limited in His ability to answer our prayers, but He is conditional in answering our prayers. He looks at the motivation of our heart, the spiritual condition of our soul, the intent in which our request is made. He also answers according to His sovereignty. Remember, God answers to no one; He needs not our approval on any decision He makes for He is omnipotent, which means He possesses complete authority and power to do anything He chooses to do at the discretion of His will. God is also omniscient, or all-knowing. He knows the past, the present, and the future. Therefore, His decisions are based on His sovereign will and His omniscience, knowing what is in our best interest for the present and the future. It is futile to pray for anything contrary to His will and contradictory to the Word of God, the Holy Bible. Notice that I did not say it is futile to pray. God wants us to pray, and He loves to answer our prayers in a manner befitting us and for His glory. When we pray in accordance to His will and with faith to receive what we ask, nothing is too grand for Him to grant it and nothing is too big that He cannot handle it.

I have entitled this book *Prayer Can Move Your Mountains: Not for the Faint of Heart* because I believe the biggest mountains we will ever face are that of self, sin, selfish pride, and a broken desire to have it our way. It is not for the faint of heart, for the request of the prayers in this book are life-altering, challenging, many times risky, but always rewarding. You will read not only the prayers from the Word of God, but also testimonies in my life of answered prayers.

It is my sincere hope and prayer for the readers of this book to enjoin themselves with the will of God for their lives and to discover the secret for answered prayer. Read this book with a teachable heart and a pliable spirit and hold on for one of the most exciting journeys of your life; God is about to *move your mountains.*

CHAPTER 1:
REMOVE YOUR MOUNTAIN
OF UNANSWERED PRAYER

The key to answered prayer is found in John 15:7: "If you abide in me and my words abide in you, you shall ask what you will, and it shall be done unto you" (KJV).

"If you live in Me (abide vitally united to Me) and My words remain in you (and continue to live in your hearts, I command you to) ask (at once) whatever you will and (even if it has to be created) it shall be done unto you" Amp. V). *If* is a little word with a big meaning; it qualifies the one praying for answered prayer. Jesus is teaching in John chapter 15 that He is the true vine and we are the branches. A limb severed from a tree cannot produce fruit and will wither and die. Jesus tells us here that apart from Him, we can do nothing. The only way we can produce fruit and receive answered prayer is to remain in Jesus and His words remain in us. Just as any electrical appliance cannot work separated from the power source, neither can we be empowered to live the Christian life or have answered prayers apart from Christ and His words.

Today's power cords have three prongs: one for the positive, one for the negative, and one for the ground wire. The first prong of our power source is Jesus. How does one come to Christ? The process is simple: whosoever will, may come. You first must come to Jesus by believing that He is the Christ, the Son of God, and that He died on the cross for your sins, was buried, and arose from the dead. The belief that brings you into Christ is more than accepting facts about a historical figure; it is belief that surrenders all of your life to His Lordship. Paul said it this way in Romans 10:9–10, "That if thou shalt confess with thy mouth the Lord Jesus, and believe in thine heart that God hath raised him from the dead, thou shalt be saved. For with the heart man believeth unto righteousness; and with the mouth confession is made unto salvation" (KJV).

How can you expect God to answer your prayers if you don't believe in His Son? It is impossible without belief. You cannot have access to the Father except by the Son. John 14:6 says, "Jesus saith unto him, 'I am the way, and the truth, and the life: no man cometh to the Father but by me'" (KJV). To be in Christ is not only to have accepted Him as your personal Lord and Savior; it is to be in His mindset, in His will. "Let this mind be in you, which was also in Christ Jesus" (Philippians 2:5 KJV).

Every day, we are to take on the character and nature of Jesus in our lives. The more we can emulate His life, the more we will be in the center of His will. It ought to be among our goals to learn to think, talk, and walk like Jesus. His desires ought to be our desires; His will our will. In short, we ought to be a Christian, one who not only claims Christ but has Christ within.

The words of Christ make up the second prong of the power cord. Jesus is the Word *(Logos)* and the "words" in John 15:7 is *rhemata,* derived from the root word *rhema,* the activated word of Christ. Christ is saying that we need to be in Him the Logos and to allow the words, rhemata, to be activated in us; that is, we need to permeate our being with the words of God and put them into action. His Holy Bible has been preserved for us in written form. We are to study, memorize, and apply the words of Christ to our lives. As the rhemata becomes a part of our life, the Holy Spirit will bring individual Scripture to our remembrance. These words have been preserved for us to keep our wants in check, so we do not ask amiss for selfish gain. They have also been preserved so that we may know the perfect will of God and His plan for our lives. As you immerse yourselves in the Word of God, you will find it to be the progressive revelation of God. He will reveal to you what you need as you need it. That is why you can read a passage of Scripture and understand it one way, and the Lord can speak to you an entirely different message the next time you study it. The rhemata completes the circuit of the power flow from Christ to man.

The third prong of our power cord is us. We are not part of the power current from God, but we are the grounding aspect of that power flow. Another way for us to understand what Christ says in John 15:7 is to think of our relationship of being in Him as our upward flow and His words being in us as His downward and inward flow. Now, because of our connection with both Him and His words, we can be better equipped to understand His will. When we have mastered the concept of being in Christ and His words being in us, we are commanded to ask at once whatever we desire, and it will be done unto us even if it has to be created. Wow, what an awesome God we serve. Think about the offer Christ has given us: unlimited access to His power, love beyond measure, constant access to His personal attention, and the command to ask what we will; even if it has to be created, He will do it for us. Remember, the key is being in Him and His words being in us.

THE POWER FLOW FOR ANSWERED PRAYER

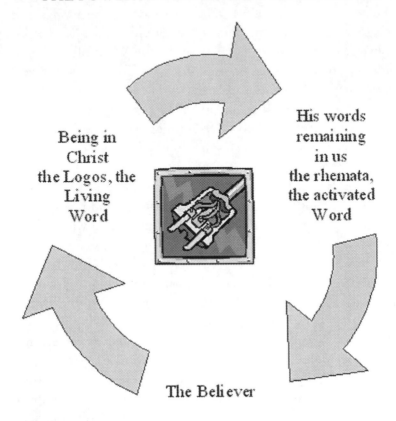

**His words
remaining
in us
the rhemata,
the activated
Word**

**Being in
Christ
the Logos, the
Living
Word**

The Believer

John 15:7 "'If ye abide in me, and my words abide in you, ye shall ask what ye will, and it shall be done unto you.'"

Several years ago, I was on a mission trip to Mexico. We were staying in a dorm in Fabians, Texas, and driving across the border each day. We were a large group and had three different teams going to our mission stations. My team came back across the border about 1:00 PM. When we arrived, our leader had misplaced the keys to one of the vans and the balance of our mission trip money ($1,500). This was the money we had to get home on. He retraced his steps, and everyone in the group looked for the money and the keys. The boys' side of the dorm was searched thoroughly, as was the girls' side, the kitchen, and the dining area. The money and keys were nowhere to be found.

I went into the restroom, into one of the stalls (funny where God will show up), and I began to pray. I told the Lord that our leader was sick and worried because he had lost the money and keys. I quoted John 15:7 to God and then prayed, "God, will you please help us find the money and the keys for our leader's sake? Lord, even if you have to re-create the money and keys." I thanked the Lord for listening to my prayer. As I was exiting the bathroom, on the top bunk bed just outside the bathroom door, I saw the money and the keys lying in plain sight. I promptly picked them up, found our leader, and gave them to him. He began to cry and thanked me for finding them. I wasn't the one to thank, God was. I don't know if we were blinded to the money and keys lying there, or if God had re-created them. All I know is we searched the dorm thoroughly, and they had not been there.

Another reason for unanswered prayer in our lives is sin. "But your iniquities have separated between you and your God, and your sins have hid his face from you, that He will not hear" (Isaiah 59:2 KJV). If you have taken that first step to become a Christian and you are in Christ and His words are in you and you are still not seeing answered prayers in your life, it is time to take an inward look. Are there hidden and unconfessed sins in your life? You cannot pray right until you get right with God. The only way to get right with God is found in 1 John 1:9 (KJV), "If we confess our sins He is faithful and just to forgive us our sins and to cleanse us from all unrighteousness." Confession is not informing God of our sins; it is agreeing with Him that we understand we have sinned. When we confess our sins, He is faithful, meaning He will forgive over and over. There is no limit to His forgiveness. He is also just: He knows when we mean business. He knows when we are truly repentant. Prayer is hindered when we harbor sin and do not confess or repent of it. Thus, many times we miss out on God's answered prayers because of sin in our lives. To remove the mountain of unanswered prayers in your life, begin by inviting Jesus into your heart to be the Lord of your life. If you have already done so, confess any known sin and ask God to forgive you and restore you to a right relationship with Him. God is merciful and gracious. He will abundantly pardon. Now, ask God to reveal to you any unknown sin in your life. Confess each sin until you have peace with God and yourself. God will remove your mountain of unanswered prayers.

REMOVE YOUR MOUNTAIN OF UNANSWERED PRAYER

Question 1. Are you in Jesus Christ?

a. If your answer is yes, write out your personal testimony of your salvation experience below.

_____

_____

_____

_____

b. If your answer is no, take this time to invite Jesus into your life. Pray the "A.B.C." prayer of salvation. A stands for admit, B stands for believe, and C stands for confess.

"Dear Lord Jesus, I admit that I am a sinner and that I cannot save myself. I believe that You are the Christ, the Son of God: that You died on a cross for my sins, that You arose from the dead, and that You live today. I confess that You are the One and only Lord and that it is only through You that I can be saved. I now invite You into my heart to be the Lord of my life. Thank You for hearing my prayer and for coming into my heart. In Your Name I pray, amen."

Question 2. How well do you know The- Holy Bible? Circle one:
            None,   Fair,   Well,   Very Well

Know the Book,.

1. There are two divisions in the Book: The Old Testament and the New Testament.

2. There are thirty-nine books in the Old Testament and twenty-seven books in the New Testament.

3. The Old Testament can be divided thus

Five Books of the Law

Genesis
Exodus
Leviticus
Numbers
Deuteronomy

Twelve Books of History

Joshua	2 Kings
Judges	1 Chronicles
Ruth	2 Chronicles
1 Samuel	Ezra
2 Samuel	Nehemiah
1 Kings	Esther

Five Books of Poetry

Job
Psalms
Proverbs
Ecclesiastes
Song of Solomon

Five Books of Major Prophets

Isaiah
Jeremiah
Lamentations
Ezekiel
Daniel

Twelve Minor Prophets

Hosea	Nahum

Joel   Habakkuk
Amos   Zephaniah
Obadiah   Haggai
Jonah   Zechariah
Micah   Malachi

4.   The New Testament can be divided thus:
Four Gospels
Matthew
Mark
Luke
John

One Book of History
Acts of the Apostles

Thirteen Pauline Epistles

Romans   1 Thessalonians
1 Corinthians   2 Thessalonians
2 Corinthians   1 Timothy
Galatians   2 Timothy
Ephesians   Titus
Philippians   Philemon
Colossians

Eight General Epistles

Hebrews   1 John
James   2 John
1 Peter   3 John
2 Peter   Jude

One Book of Apocalypse
Revelation

b. Memorize the Word

    1.   List the verses you have committed to memory.

    _____

    _____

    _____

    2.   The rhemata is the activated Word of God. List below one way you know that the Word is activated in your life. Back it up with Scripture. Example: 1 Thessalonians 5:18: "In every thing give thanks; for this is the will of God in Christ Jesus concerning you."

I acknowledge that every good and perfect gift comes from above and I do give thanks for all that God has blessed me with. Even in the bad things that happen in my life I give thanks for the presence of the Lord in my life.

    _____

    _____

    _____

    _____

    _____

In the following chapters, you will be given Scripture verses that will deal with the particular issue of the chapter to memorize and apply when and where needed. As you memorize a verse, come back to this chapter and add them to your list of memorized verses.

Prayer Challenge:
"Dear Lord, I have given my life to You and accepted You into my heart. I want to please You with my life, so please Lord reveal any un-confessed sin in my life so that I may agree with You that it is sin and help me to overcome that sin in my life. Please help me to learn, memorize Your Word, and apply it to my life. Let Your Word become active in and through me. In the precious name of Jesus I pray, amen."

CHAPTER 2:
REMOVE YOUR MOUNTAIN
OF UNBELIEF

Nothing cripples your prayer life like unbelief. If I surveyed every Christian in your church and asked them how many of them believed in Jesus, 100 percent would say they do. If I asked them how many believe God can do anything, again, 100 percent would say they do. If I asked them if God can heal, raise the dead, create life, and still the wind and waves, again, 100 percent would say He can. Then why are there are so many unanswered prayers? I believe Jesus is still asking, "Why are you so fearful? How is it that you have no faith?" Our problem is not that we don't believe God can, our problem is having faith that He will answer our prayers.

Faith in the smallest amount results in moving mountains. If you are a Christian, you are a person of faith, for it is impossible to be a Christian without it. Ephesians 2:8–9 says, "For by grace are you saved through faith, and that not of yourselves, it is the gift of God. Not of works lest any man should boast." We are in both a physical world and a spiritual world. To be saved, or come to Christ, one has to have had a breakthrough from thinking in the physical realm. He has realized there is more to life than the physical; he understands that they have a soul and that soul will go on living after the physical life has ended. By faith, he believed in a Jesus whom he has not seen. He has accepted by faith His vicarious death for him. In his simple, childlike faith, one mountain has already been removed in his life: the mountain of the penalty and bondage of sin. Becoming a Christian does not mean that you are instantly a mature Christian. Faith is a process of growth; the more you exercise it the deeper it grows and matures. Paul is a wonderful example of a person growing in faith. "Not that I speak in respect of want: for I have learned, in whatsoever state I am, therewith to be content" (Philippians 4:11 KJV). Lessons in life are learned, and lessons in growing in faith are learned as well. *Each time God answers a prayer in your life, journal it. Each time doubt rises in your heart, go back and read your journal.* Recollection of God's answered prayers, His unexpected blessings that come your way, and His provision for your daily needs will help you grow in your faith.

I love the story in Mark 9:14–29 of a father who comes to Jesus' disciples with a son who has seizures and is unable to speak. They cannot solve the problem and then they bring the boy to Jesus. When Jesus is told about the boy, he rebukes the disciples in verse 19: "'You unbelieving generation! How long will I be with you? How long must I put up with you? Bring him to Me.' So they brought him to Him. When the spirit saw Him, it immediately convulsed the boy. He fell to the ground and rolled around, foaming at the mouth. 'How long has this been happening to him?' Jesus asked his father. 'From childhood,' he said. 'And many times it has thrown him into fire or water to destroy him. But if You can do anything, have compassion on us and help us.' Then Jesus said to him, 'If You can? Everything is possible to the one who believes.' Immediately the father of the boy cried out, 'I do believe! Help my unbelief.' When Jesus saw that a crowd was rapidly coming together, He rebuked the unclean spirit, saying to it, 'You mute and deaf spirit, I command you: come out of him and never enter him again.' Then it came out, shrieking and convulsing him violently. The boy became like a corpse, so that many said, 'He's dead.' But Jesus, taking him by the hand, raised him, and he stood up" (CSV).

The next step toward removing your mountain of unbelief is to admit that even as a believer, you struggle with unbelief. Ask God to help you with your unbelief. Take Jesus at His word when He said, "Everything is possible to the one who believes." Unbelief does not trust the Lord. Ask the Lord to strengthen your faith. Simply ask Him to remove your mountain of unbelief.

Since I have gone into full-time evangelism, I have had to exercise faith. When I told my wife that God was calling me into full-time evangelism after thirty-two years of being a pastor, Glenda replied, "Charlie, for thirty-six years I have trusted you to do what the Lord has told you to do, and if you believe God is leading you into full-time evangelism, I'm in." We made a pact that we would not borrow money and that we would trust God to take care of us. Time after time, the Lord came through for us. Our faith has grown by leaps and bounds, but even now there are times that unbelief creeps back into our lives. One month we did not have the money to make our mortgage payment, and I told Glenda that I was going to the bank to borrow the money to make the payment. She told me in unequivocal terms that we were not going to borrow the money, but that we were going to trust God to provide. I confessed my unbelief, and we got down by our bed and prayed for the Lord to take care of our need. The next morning, I went to the post office and found a check for $1,000 in my mailbox. It was from a family that I had pastored twenty-three years before. Linda, the wife of that family, told us that her father had left her an inheritance and that she was sending a one-time gift of the thousand dollars. God taught us a valuable lesson about faith. How is yours about now? You can trust God to take care of you.

Unbelief transcends our belief in God, or lack thereof; unbelief affects our own being as well. Most Christians I know believe and trust God, but too many Christians do not believe in themselves.

For those who have been beaten down, live in guilt, or who have inferiority complexes, unbelief in their ability to live the Christian life is a natural result. They have forgotten who they are in Jesus Christ. They see the life of a Christian as a burden rather than a joy. With unrealistic expectations of themselves, they live defeated lives. They are unhappy, disillusioned, broken, and burdened with the idea they have to live it alone. For this very reason, there are several Scriptures that remind us of who we are in Christ, and that we are not in this alone. "But to as many as received Him to them gave He power to become sons of God, even to them who believe on His name" (John 1:12). Here, the Word reveals to us that we have been given power to become children of God. We live the life of a Christian not in our own strength, but in God's. Paul had an infirmity that he had prayed God would remove. He was weak and broken until the Lord spoke to him and said in II Corinthians 12:9: "And He said unto me, 'My grace is sufficient for thee: for my strength is made perfect in weakness.' Most gladly therefore will I rather glory in my infirmities, that the power of Christ may rest upon me. Therefore I take pleasure in infirmities, in reproaches, in necessities, in persecutions, in distresses for Christ's sake: for when I am weak, then am I strong" (KJV). If you are a Christian and you don't have much confidence in yourself, here is a simple formula that will help: trust in His ability, rather than your inability, through your availability to do what only He can do through you. "I can do all things through Christ who strengthens me" (Philippians 4:13).

Ask God to reveal to you His presence in your life. Tell him how inadequate you feel in yourself and ask Him to give you courage and boldness to do far and above anything you ever believed possible. Confidence comes when we realize that the Christian life is only lived when Christ lives in and through us.

REMOVE YOUR MOUNTAIN OF UNBELIEF

Question 1. In what areas of your life are you struggling to trust the Lord?

  a. Spiritual e. Job security
  b. Financial f. Future
  c. Health   g. Retirement
  d. Family   h. Church

Question 2. When was the last time your faith was challenged?

_____

_____

Question 3. On a scale of one to ten, ten being the best, how do you rate your faith that your daily prayers will be answered?

_____

Question 4. Is your faith strong enough to handle God's answer of no? _____ Can you, along with Paul, say, "God's grace is sufficient for me"? _____

Question 5. Can you be honest enough with yourself and God to admit that your belief and faith are weak and you need His help to strengthen your faith? _____

Prayer Challenge:
"Our Father, I admit there are times my faith is weak and I do need You to strengthen my faith. Help me to know when Your answer is no or be spiritually discerning enough to know my faith is weak concerning what I am praying about. Help me to always remember that You always hear my prayers and that You will never leave me nor forsake me. Amen."

Hebrews 13:5: "Let your conduct be without covetousness; be content with such things as you have. For He Himself has said, 'I will never leave you nor forsake you.'"

CHAPTER 3:
REMOVE YOUR MOUNTAIN OF WEAKNESS AND SIN

This chapter is not for the faint of heart; it will rock you to your bones. The prayer of David in Psalm 26:2 is by far one of the boldest prayers written in the Bible. When you understand the implications of this prayer, it is definitely life-changing. "Examine me, O Lord, and prove me, try my reigns and my heart" (Psalm 26:2 KJV). This prayer is short, simple, and to the point. David is asking for something that few will dare pray. If you will pray this prayer with conviction, honesty, and submission to God's answer, your life will never be the same again.

I have read motivational books, heard motivational speakers, and conducted motivational seminars. As good as they are, none can change a life for the better like this single prayer. This prayer deals with our shortcomings, our steel, God's control of our lives, and the motivation of our hearts.

Tests are necessary to reveal what we have learned, both in school and in life. They are not always pleasant and sometimes can be very difficult. Tests reveal our weaknesses as well as our strengths. In school, when you miss a question on a test, the idea is to go back and learn from your mistake. In life, when we fail the tests, we need to learn from our mistakes as well. Thomas Edison failed thousands of times before he got the incandescent light bulb right. Failing a test is only failure when you fail to learn from your mistakes. When the Lord puts you through a test, it is to build you up and never intended to make you fall. It reveals the areas of your life that need improving. God's tests are sometimes very difficult to accept, and many times you will fail, but rest assured that He will be there to pick you up, set you on solid ground, and help you succeed. God's tests are not generally solicited; most often they come as a surprise. What makes this prayer so bold is that David solicited God to test him. What did David know that we fail to understand? Why would anyone solicit a test from God? Could it be that David would rather be under God's microscope than man's? Think about how mankind judges one another. Man has only the example of others to judge you by. He has not walked where you have walked. He cannot know the circumstances that have lead up to the decisions you have made in life. God, on the other hand, has been there in every step you have made, every circumstance that you have ever experienced, and He even knows every thought you have ever had. Another reason David wanted God to be the one to examine him was that there is no one more fair or perfect than God. God will have no selfish motive in His judgment and his decisions will be just. When we come under the Lord's microscope, he reveals our weakness and has the ability to correct our errors.

Several years ago, I went through the program called Master Life. The program ended with a prayer retreat. Our last assignment was to pray for four hours. I thought there was no way I could pray for four hours. I began my prayer of praise, which I thought would take the first hour, but after about fifteen minutes I had exhausted my thank-you list. I then thought, only three hours and forty-five minutes to go. Then I decided to ask God to reveal my unconfessed sins and weaknesses. I agreed that every sin that God revealed to me was sin, repented, and moved on to the next one. I also confessed agreement with every weakness God revealed about my character and heart and then I asked Him to help me overcome my weakness.

The next three hours and forty-five minutes flew by. Don't ever pray for God to reveal your sin and weakness to you unless you're ready to do business with God. I promise you God will deal with those areas of your life. No wonder David asked God to put him to the test. God is the only one qualified to do so.

The second part of the prayer deals with God proving us. This concept is the same as a refiner burning off the distaff in gold. When we are refined, that is, when we are put through the fire of God, the impurities in our lives are burnt up and only the purest gold of our character remains. When God puts you through His refinery, it will test your steel, what you are made of, and I promise it will make you into a better person than you ever dreamed possible.

As I mentioned earlier, after thirty-two years in the pastorate, God called me into full-time evangelism. For me this was a great thrill because I knew I was in the center of God's will. Glenda, on the other hand, who had been a pastor's wife for so many years, felt that her ministry had been taken from her. She couldn't teach or lead a ladies' Bible study class anymore because of our traveling schedule. She asked me to pray that God would give her a ministry that she could share as we traveled across the country and around the world. Six weeks later, Glenda was in a terrible riding accident. We had just gotten a new horse and thought it had been broken, but it hadn't. On the day before Easter 2009, Glenda's best friend Ruth and Dr. Robin Stevenson were with us to see the new horse. I put Ruth on the horse and he did fine. Then Glenda got on the horse, and she said the saddle was loose, so I cinched the saddle up tight, and the rodeo was on. The horse bucked up his front quarters, and Glenda went all the way back on him until her head hit his rump. Then he kicked up his hind quarters and she came all the way forward and hit her face on the saddle horn. She was knocked unconscious, and the horse repeated his bucking until she hit the saddle horn a second time and fell off. She fell on her back, bleeding out of her eyes, her nose, and her mouth. All the bones in her face had been broken. As she lay on the ground, I thought she was either dead or in the process of dying. Our doctor friend did not think she was going to make it either. While Ruth was on the phone with 911, a man pulled into our driveway, jumped out of his car with a medical bag, took out a piece of gauze, and placed it on Glenda's nose, where a piece of bone had come through. He said that the first responders would be there soon, and as he spoke those words, they pulled into our driveway. As the paramedics knelt over Glenda, I turned to say something to the man who had placed the gauze on her nose and he was gone, and so was his car. The ambulance came and took Glenda to our local hospital, and after her CAT scan, the emergency room doctor told me her nose was broken and that she had a brain contusion. I told him that her teeth didn't look right to me and he checked her by pulling on her front teeth and the whole center of her face moved. He said she was seriously hurt and needed to go immediately to Tulsa and have surgery on her face. He said he knew of a doctor by the name of Dr. Paul Howard in Tulsa that he believed was the best at facial reconstruction. Dr. Howard took Glenda's case, and after more CAT scans, he decided it would be better to wait until morning to do her surgery to make sure her brain didn't swell. The surgery took about three and a half hours on Easter Sunday. Dr. Howard told me that he had to put a plate in her face in the shape of a cross, that her teeth would be wired shut for thirty days, and that she would have a tracheal tube (trach) in for forty days. After surgery, Glenda was in intensive care for four days and then in the hospital for another five. Today you cannot tell she was ever in an accident except for the small scar where her trach was. As the result of her testimony since the accident, hundreds of people have been encouraged and at least seventeen people have come to know Jesus as their personal savior. When I thanked Dr. Howard for taking such good care of Glenda, he told me, "I do the doctoring, but the Lord does the healing."

This was a huge test of fire for Glenda, and me, but the rewards of going through the test were worth it. I wouldn't put Glenda back through the test for anything, but I also wouldn't take back the experience of going through it. Glenda will tell you that it was worth it if only one person had been saved as the result of her testimony.

Asking God to prove you doesn't mean that you will have to go through something like what Glenda went through, but when God puts you through His fire, the purest of your character will shine through.

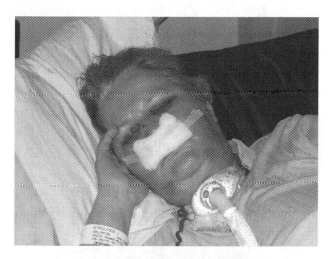

Top photo is of Glenda in the hospital. The bottom photo is of Glenda six weeks after getting out of the hospital.

21

The next part of the prayer says, "Try my reins." Reins are the controlling factor in horseback riding. David was asking God to reveal how much control He had of his life. Too often we want to be in control of our lives and do not relinquish our will to God's will. When this happens, we get stiff-necked, stubborn, and end up making mistakes in our lives. When we relinquish our will to His, our lives run more smoothly and more happily.

Just out of high school, my parents moved to Pond Creek, Oklahoma, where Dad was pastor of the First Baptist Church. A man in the church told me he had a horse I could ride that he kept at the fairground barn and that I could go down and ride him anytime I wanted to. I took him up on his offer and saddled the horse and then rode to our house. No one told me the horse was barn sour. A barn sour horse is one that gets fed in the barn and wants to run back to the barn in order to be fed. When I turned the horse back toward the barn, the horse began running. I thought, *Boy, I like running.* That was, until I looked up and saw that between me and the barn was a highway with semi trucks going back and forth. I told the horse to whoa, but he kept on running. I pulled back on the reins and shouted to whoa again, but he just stiffened his neck and kept on running. I didn't know what else to do but to double my fist; I pulled his head up and struck him between his ears. He stopped dead in his tracks. I just had to get his attention.

When we ask God to reveal His control of our lives to us, it will prevent Him from having to get our attention. If you will ask God to reveal any area of your life that you have not yielded to Him, He will. Then confess that area of your life and submit it to His will.

The final part of the prayer is to ask God to reveal your heart to you. To reveal your heart is to reveal the essence of who you are, what makes you tick. It is the motivational factor of your life. We can want the right thing in life but for the wrong reason. We can reveal truth, but if it is revealed for the purpose of hurting someone, then the motive is wrong. We can go to church, but if our motive is to see who is wearing what, to get in on the latest gossip, or to impress someone with how spiritual we are, our motive is wrong. A wrong motive can hinder blessings, quench the Spirit, and even be destructive to you and others. It is vitally important for God to reveal the motivational factor of our lives for Him to be able to work both in us and through us.

Look at this prayer with all four parts in mind:

1. "Examine me O Lord"—test me.

2. "Prove me"—put me through the fire and burn off or take away the trash in my life.

3. "Try my reins"—show me the controlling factor of my life.

4. "And my heart"—reveal the motivational factor of my life.

Be bold enough to pray this prayer and sit back and see what God will do through your committed, submissive life.

Charles F. Keim

REMOVE YOUR MOUNTAIN
OF WEAKNESS AND SIN

Question 1. Why should you ask God to put you through a test?

_____

_____

Remember, God is omnipresent; He is everywhere. He has been
there your entire life. He is omniscient; He is all-knowing. He
knows why you have lived the way you have. He understands you
even more than you do. He is omnipotent; He is all-powerful.
There is nothing that God cannot do but lie.

Question 2. Are you wise enough to learn from your mistakes?

_____

Name one mistake you have made in your life that taught you a
lesson. (Make sure the mistake you write down is one that you
wouldn't mind the world to know about. There may be some
mistakes that you have made that are better left between you and
God.)

_____

_____

_____

_____

_____

Question 3. In David's prayer he said, "prove me," or another way
of saying that is "put me through the refiner's fire." A refiner burns
off the distaff from gold ore. When we ask God to put us through
the fire, we are asking Him to take the trash out of our lives. We
are asking Him to purify our lives. What trash needs to be taken
from your life? Make a list of things you need to be taken from
your life in order for God to purify you.

24

_____

_____

_____

_____

Question 4. When David asked the Lord to try his reins, he was asking God to reveal how much control He had of his life. How much control does God have of your life? List areas of your life that you need to relinquish to the Lord.

_____

_____

_____

_____

Question 5. The final part of David's prayer asks God to try his heart. It is from your heart that you reveal the truth of who you are and what it is that motivates your actions. What is the motivational factor for your life?

_____

_____

Question 6. Is your service for God and others from pure motives or from selfish motives?

_____

Question 7. Is the motivational factor of your life in line with God's will for your life? Are your priorities right in your life? List below the areas of your life where your priorities are out of order.

_____

_____

_____

_____

Now list how you believe the Lord would have you align your priorities.

_____

_____

_____

_____

Some people base their service to God out of fear that they will lose their salvation; my motivational factor in my service to God is out of love and appreciation for what He has already done in and through my life. Make sure you get your priorities right and serve God with a pure heart.

CHAPTER 4:
REMOVE YOUR
MOUNTAIN OF FEAR

Fear terrorizes the faint-hearted. It quiets the message of Jesus Christ. It robs the believer of a victorious Christian life. It quenches the Spirit. It retreats when one should be on the offense. It hides in silence and seclusion when the believer should be set on a lamp stand as a light to the world. Fear can even rob a nonbeliever of his soul by cowering from the Lord's call, fearing what people will think. Fearing what may be asked of him as a believer. Fearing not being able to live the Christian life, and the list goes on and on. No wonder the Bible tells us over six hundred times to "fear not." Fear kept Israel out of the Promised Land for forty years. Fear is the opposite of faith. Fear keeps one from living. How in the world do you conquer fear?

Many times, fear is the result of false perception. Ten of the twelve spies that went into the Promised Land saw themselves as grasshoppers compared to the men in Canaan, whom they saw as giants. The result was that Israel wandered in the wilderness for forty years. Peter walked on the water until he took his eyes off of Jesus and listened to the wind and the waves. I ask again, how do you conquer fear?

God tells Isaiah, in Isaiah 41:10, how to conquer fear. "Fear not, for I am with thee, be not dismayed for I am thy God, I will strengthen thee, yea, I will help thee, yea, I will uphold thee with the right hand of my righteousness" (KJV).

The first step in conquering fear is to obey God. He said, "Fear not." That is a direct command from God. "For you have not received the spirit of bondage again to fear; but you have received the Spirit of adoption, whereby we cry, Abba Father" (Romans 8:15 KJV). When we accept Jesus into our hearts, we are born again and receive the Spirit of adoption into the family of God. Two things have happened when one gives his life to Christ. First, they are born again. Read John chapter 3. Being born into God's family makes us joint heirs with Jesus Christ Himself. We are now His children under our Father's love, protection, provision, and instruction. When Paul said we have been given the Spirit of adoption, he simply means that we can never be disowned. When a believer truly understands we have a heavenly Father who loves us unconditionally, it changes our perspective on how we view the world and all the terrible things that go on in this world.

The second step in conquering fear is to understand that God is with us. "Fear not for I am with you;" You are never alone. If you understand that God is with you, you can face any trial that comes your way. Having God with us doesn't mean things will never go wrong in our lives, but it does mean that God will never abandon us and He will be with us through it all.

When Glenda, my wife, had her horse riding accident and I saw her lying on the ground, I thought I was seeing my wife pass away right before my eyes. All of a sudden I realized I was not alone. A tremendous awareness of God's presence was with me and a peace flooded my soul. What blessed assurance we have to know God is with us.

The third step in conquering fear is to understand the awesome power of God. "Fear not, for I am with thee, be not dismayed for I am thy God" The word *dismayed* is an interesting word. It carries a plethora of meanings. It means distressed, disappointed, distraught, troubled, sad, in a state, in tears, saddened, wounded, offended. Again, we have a direct command here to not be dismayed, distressed, disappointed, distraught, troubled, sad, in a state, in tears, saddened, wounded, or offended because "I am thy God." The *I am* tells us God exists. God is the essence of being. It was the name given to Moses at the burning bush: "tell them, I Am has sent you." We need no other description of God than to know He is the essence of being. *Thy God* tells us that He is our personal God. When I was in college, I had a professor tell us one day that God is not a personal God. I responded that anyone who says that God is not a personal God is not someone who knows Him, nor do they know the Word. God could not have been any clearer here with His revelation that He is a personal God. When we can wrap around the meaning and essence of God and His awesome power, it changes our perspective on how big we see our mountains of fear. God is omnipresent; He is everywhere. "Whither shall I go from thy spirit? Or whither shall I flee from thy presence? If I ascend up into heaven, thou art there: if I make my bed in hell, behold, thou art there. If I take the wings of the morning, and dwell in the uttermost parts of the sea; Even there shall thy hand lead me, and thy right hand shall hold me" (Psalm 139:7–10 KJV). There is no place you can go that God will not already be there. He is omniscient, all-knowing. He knows the past, the present, and the future. He is omnipotent; He has unlimited power and authority. God can do anything but fail.

When I was a senior in college, I had been to a state evangelism conference and heard a young preacher by the name of Richard Douglas, who was pastor of Putnam City Baptist Church. I was so impressed with his preaching ability and charisma. Not long after that, he and his wife were murdered in their home, and his children left for dead. When I heard that news, it made me sick to my stomach, bewildered, and fearful. I thought, how could God let something happen to such a wonderful man as Richard Douglas? I prayed and asked God why He allowed that to happen. God gave me the answer in Isaiah 41:10. After I read that verse,

God told me, "Charlie, I know what I am doing. Trust me." I knew from that moment on that God was in control, and my fear went away. You can trust God to move your mountain of fear. Pray and obey. That is it; pray for God to help you obey His command to not fear and to help you trust Him to understand that He is absolutely in control. Back in the '50s, there was a TV show called *Father Knows Best*, starring Robert Young. In real life, our heavenly Father does know best, for all of us. *Trust Him, don't be afraid.*

REMOVE YOUR
MOUNTAIN OF FEAR

Question 1. What makes you fearful? Circle your answers below.

Unknown	Crowds	Heights
Darkness	Being Alone	Death
God's Judgement	End of Time	God's Will
Heaven	Hell	Illness
World Events	Weather	Failure
Rejection	Other	Other

Question 2. What do you fear in your life that is bigger and stronger than God? _____

Question 3. Why do you think it was necessary for God to put in His word over six hundred times to "not fear"?

_____

_____

_____

Prayer Challenge:
"Our Father, I know that You love me and want what is best for me. I owe my life and my soul to You. I am but human with human frailties, I am subject to hurts and pains, space and time, life and death, yet I know that You are in control. Help me to not fear but to trust You with every area of my life. I do believe You are the one and only God who can do anything You so desire. I praise You for being my creator, the sustainer of my life, the provider of my needs, and the keeper of my spirit. Help me to be brave in spirit, mighty in prayer, and ever faithful to You, my Lord and my God. In the name of Your precious Son, Jesus Christ, amen."

Chapter 5:
Remove Your
Mountain of Guilt

There is a world of difference between humility and guilt. Humility can make one quiet, submissive, and sometimes even passive. But guilt disables to the point of brokenness, uselessness, reclusiveness, shame, and many times, depression. The burden of guilt can weigh one down to the point of suicide. How tragic it is for a person to go through life with the burden of guilt on his shoulders. Even more tragic is when a Christian can accept Christ's forgiveness of his sins, but not forgive himself. Every person deals with guilt once in a while, but to have pronounced yourself guilty to the point of no return is deplorable. When a believer will not forgive himself, he makes a mockery of the forgiveness of God. In essence, he is saying to God, "You just don't know what you are doing." Listen, God knows your past, present, and future and He still loves you. "For when we were still without strength, in due time Christ died for the ungodly. God demonstrated His love to us, even while we were still sinners, Christ died for us" (Romans 5:6, 8 NKJV).

All through the ages, man has felt the guilt of sin. Adam and Eve hid in the Garden of Eden. Moses hid a body in the desert and fled to the back side of the wilderness. King David sinned with Bathsheba and covered his adulterous affair by having her husband, Uriah, killed in battle. Paul said he was the chief of all sinners. David gives us the clearest example of all those mentioned above in how to get rid of the guilt of sin. Psalm 51 is his confession and prayer of renewal. First, David asked God for His mercy and this according to His attribute of loving kindness. Three things David asked God to do about his sin:

1. "Blot out my transgressions" (Psalm 51:1c CSV). David was asking God to totally remove the transgression from him. Transgression is a violation of a law or code. David had broken the commandments of God.

2. "Wash me thoroughly from my iniquity" (Psalm 51:2a CSV). Iniquity is an immoral act. Here he asked God to wash him from the immoral act.

3. "Cleanse me from my sin" (Psalm 51:2b). Finally, he asked God to cleanse him from his sin. Sin is a shameful offense against God.

If your guilt is the result of a transgression, that is, if you have broken a commandment, ask God to blot it out of your life. If you have committed an immoral act, ask God to wash you from that iniquity, and if you have sinned, ask God to cleanse you of your sin. Think about what you have asked God to do for you, blot the transgression out, wash away the iniquity, and cleanse you from the sin. I have great news for you: I John 1:9 says, "If we confess our sins, He is faithful and just to forgive us our sins and to cleans us from all unrighteousness" (KJV). In this verse we see that our forgiveness and cleansing is conditional. There is that *if* word again. It is conditional on our confession. Confession is not informing God of your failure, but agreeing with Him. There are two things about the nature of God here: God is faithful and God is just. Remember, God is omniscient; He knows your sincerity and your heart. If you are sincere with your confession, He will be faithful to cleanse you every time. But if you are not sincere, He is also just, and you will not enjoy the freedom of being cleansed.

When I was just out of high school, I went through a rebellious time in my life. I partied and was silent about my relationship with Christ. I would kneel by my bed each night and tell God how sorry I was for what I had done that day. God would promptly tell me that I was not sorry and I was not repentant because I was going to do it again. This went on for several weeks until one day I said to God, "I can't stand myself; I don't want to live like this anymore. Please forgive me." God promptly replied that I was forgiven. I learned a valuable lesson from that experience. There is a big difference between regret of your action and repentance of your action. Repentance is coming to the point of having a changed heart and mind. It is a turning away from the sin in your life. God knows the difference. When you confess your sins, do so with sincerity and repentance and God will thoroughly cleanse you.

The second thing David does is deal with his own attitude and peace of mind and soul. In Psalm 51:10 David said, "Create in me a clean heart, O God; and renew a right spirit within me" (KJV). And in verse 12 he said, "Restore unto me the joy of thy salvation; and uphold me with thy free spirit" (KJV). After you have taken your transgressions, iniquities, and sins to God through Christ Jesus, ask Him to create a new heart in you that is cleansed and to renew a right spirit within you. A right spirit will result in a right attitude. When you are cleansed and you know it, you will be guilt free. When you are freed from your guilt, God will return the joy of your salvation.

The apostle John tells us in I John 3:20, "For if our hearts condemn us, God is greater than our heart, and knoweth all things. Beloved, if our hearts condemn us not, then we have confidence toward God" (KJV).

John is telling us in verse twenty that if we have been forgiven by God but still carry guilt in our heart, that God is greater than our heart. It is destructive and unprofitable to carry guilt when you do not have to. When you finally get it, that you're forgiven and cleansed and your heart no longer carries the guilt, then you will have confidence toward God and be guilt free.

Where do you think the guilt comes from after you have been forgiven? It is false guilt brought on by the accuser, Satan. If Christ has forgiven you, you are no longer guilty. But Satan wants you to believe you are still guilty and unclean. He makes his accusations both day and night. Listen to what John says about that old serpent, the Devil, in Revelations 12:10: "Then I heard a loud voice in heaven say: The salvation and the power and the kingdom of our God and the authority of His Messiah have now come, because the accuser of our brothers has been thrown out: the one who accuses them before our God day and night" (CSV).

Want to be guilt free? Go for it. Have confidence in God and His cleansing power. If the Devil reminds you of your past failures and sins, you remind him of his future.

REMOVE YOUR
MOUNTAIN OF GUILT

Question 1. Do you carry a burden of guilt in your life?

_____

Question 2. If your answer is yes, have you asked Jesus to forgive you and cleanse you of that which makes you feel guilt?

_____

(If your answer is no, then ask Jesus to forgive you now of the sin that you are convicted of and invite Him into your heart.

Question 3. Do you still carry a burden of guilt after you have asked Jesus to forgive you?

_____

Question 4. If your answer to the above question is yes, what sin in your life is greater than the blood of Jesus?

_____

Question 5. I John 1:9 says, "If we confess our sins He is faithful and just to forgive us our sins and cleanse us from *all* unrighteousness" (emphasis mine). What sin in your life has not been included in the *all* in this verse?

_____

Question 6. Are you still feeling guilt in your life? _____
If your answer is yes, there are two things you can do:

1. Ask God to forgive you of doubting His ability and faithfulness to forgive and cleanse you.

2. Tell Satan to get behind you, because you have been washed clean by the blood of the Lamb, Jesus Christ.

John 8:36: "Therefore if the Son makes you free, you shall be free indeed." (Free, even of guilt.)

Prayer Challenge:
"Our Father, who art in heaven, I know You are holy and righteous in every way. When my life is compared to You, I realize how lowly I am. I am so grateful for Your love, grace, and mercy. I bring to You my sin of _____ in confession; please cleanse me of my sin. I know You already know my heart and with the best of my ability I admit and relinquish this sin to You. Please restore the joy of my salvation and help me never to repeat this sin again. In the precious name of Jesus I pray, amen."

CHAPTER 6:
REMOVE YOUR MOUNTAIN OF DOUBT

Doubt creates all kinds of problems for the doubter. It will lead to frustration, indecision, and confusion and leave you an emotional wreck. I have known believers who have been baptized over and over because of doubt. Life rocks on for them until the old accuser raises his ugly head and reminds them of how unworthy they are of God's love and salvation. He reminds them of all their past failures and sins. This kind of doubt arises out of an attitude of believing you have to earn your salvation. Even though they say they believe salvation is by grace through faith, in their heart of hearts, they believe you have to earn it. When they fail to live up to the standard they judge others by, they believe they are lost. When a Christian doubts his salvation, he is defeated in his quest for a victorious Christian life. Satan has won a battle in his life, but not the war. In the end, the Christian will realize he is truly saved and that all of his doubting has accomplished nothing.

For the doubter, it is time for a reality check. For sure, you do not want to go through life with false hope, believing you're saved when you are not. But neither do you want to go through life as a Christian believing you may be lost. That is why God gave us the book of I John. "I have written these things to you who believe in the name of the Son of God, so that you may know you have eternal life" (I John 5:13 CSV). By a careful study of I John, you can examine your life and know whether or not you have eternal life.

Our money has changed in appearance in the past few years. This has been done to protect our society from counterfeiters. Banks across America trained their employees to recognize a counterfeit bill by teaching the characteristics of the real money without once showing them a counterfeit bill. When you know the characteristics of a real Christian, you can spot imposters in no time at all. Their characteristics will give them away.

In the next few pages, we are going to look at the characteristics of a real Christian from the book of I John, prefaced by II Corinthians 5:17: "Therefore, if any man be in Christ, he is a new creature: old things are passed away; behold all things are become new" (KJV). Paul tells the Corinthians that if a person has come to faith in Jesus Christ, he or she is a new creature. There is not another one in the world exactly like the believer. He has maintained his own identity as well as taken on the identity of Jesus Christ. Old things have passed away. The old nature he was enslaved to is gone. The bondage of sin has been broken. Everything in the believer's life has changed and become new. A believer will see the world differently than a lost person. He will encompass a new realm of reality. He is no longer just in the physical world, but through Christ, he has entered a spiritual world. This new experience changes his vision; he now sees through the eyes of Christ. Things that once did not bother him now have become offensive. He perceives and views people in a different light. He sees through more compassionate eyes and perceives with a more compassionate heart. It changes his hearing; he hears through the ears of Christ. Where once he could listen to the language of the world, the cursing, the vulgar talk now offends him. Listening to the Word of God preached, read, or sung is now more pleasing to him. It changes his language; he now speaks through the tongue of Christ. Where once telling lies, bad jokes, and cursing came with no remorse, now slipping up is shocking and immediate conviction comes. In short, a born-again believer's life is radically different. John gives us litmus tests to check our salvation. John begins his argument for a changed life in I John 1:7. "But if we walk in the light, as He is in the light, we have fellowship one with another, and the blood of Jesus Christ His Son cleanses us from all sin" (KJV). Walking in the light is a metaphor for living a Christ-centered life, a righteous life, just as Christ lived and lives a righteous life. The norm for the Christian will be a desire to live like Christ. A believer will emulate the life of Christ in his own life. The result of walking in the light will be evident through the fellowship that we have with our fellow man. There is also the awareness of being cleansed of all our sin.

The second litmus test is in keeping His commandments. "He that says, I know Him, and keeps not His commandments, is a liar, and the truth is not in him. But whoever keeps His word, in him verily is the love of God perfected: by this we know we are in Him" (I John 2:4–5 NKJV). Remember, the key to answered prayer is abiding in Christ and His words abiding in us. John verifies it here. We are to be in Christ and His word is to be in us, and when there is the combination of the two, it will result in obedience.

The third litmus test is found in I John 2:20: "But you have an anointing from the Holy One, and you all know all things" (NKJV). John is telling us here that a true Christian has an anointing from the Holy One, that is, he has been given the Holy Spirit as his teacher and guide. Where, as a nonbeliever, you had a difficult time understanding the Word of God, now, as a believer, your eyes have been opened to the Word. Now there is understanding and light where once there was only darkness.

The fourth litmus test is your confession that Jesus has come in the flesh. "This is how you know the Spirit of God: Every spirit who confesses that Jesus Christ has come in the flesh is from God" (I John 4:2 CSV). This confession of Christ can only be the result of conviction of God on one's life. One confesses what he believes and, in a true Christian, that is evidenced through confessing that the Son of God came in the flesh of man.

The fifth litmus test is found in I John 5:1: "Everyone who believes that Jesus is the Messiah has been born of God, and everyone who loves the parent also loves his child" (CSV). New birth is revealed by one who believes that the Son of God came to this earth as the promised one, the Messiah and loves Him. *Belief* is the key word here. One must believe in the Son of God in order to be saved.

The sixth litmus test is that of overcoming the world. "Because, whatever has been born of God conquers the world. This is the victory that conquered the world: our faith. And who is the one who conquers the world but the one who believes that Jesus is the Son of God?" (I John 5:4–5 CSV). By faith, a believer is an overcomer. The world no longer holds him. He has been liberated.

The seventh litmus test is found in I John 5:18: "We know that everyone who has been born of God does not sin, but the One who is born of God keeps Him, and the evil one does not touch Him" (CSV). The message here is that one who is truly born again cannot continue in habitual sin. The Holy Spirit will convict him of his sin and not permit it to dominate his life.

One of the surest signs that you have been born again is an acute awareness that you have sinned immediately after the altercation. No one has to tell you that you have sinned, the Spirit that dwells in you will reveal it immediately.

If you doubt your salvation, ask yourself these questions: Am I walking in the light of Christ? Is it my desire to do what is right? Am I the happiest when I am living for Jesus? Do I desire to keep His commands? Do I desire to please God with my lifestyle? Do I understand God's Word? Has the Word of God come alive for me? When I read the Bible, do I understand what I am reading? Have I confessed my faith in Jesus that He came in the flesh? Do I believe He is the Son of God? Do I believe that Jesus is the Messiah and do I love Him? Have I overcome the world? Have I been liberated from the bondage of sin? Am I the happiest when I am living for Jesus? Do I have an awareness of sin immediately after I commit the sin? Does anyone have to tell me I have sinned?

If none of the above is a positive yes, then you may be a nonbeliever. If that is the case, ask the Lord to reveal Himself to you and confess your faith in Him; ask Him to come into your life. If you were able to answer yes to most of the above questions, then thank God for it and never doubt again.

Prayer Challenge:
"Oh, Father, I have let doubt creep into my life to the point of hindrance of living a productive Christian life. Please forgive me of my doubt, for I know when I doubt it is not me that I doubt, it is You. Give me the courage to never doubt our relationship again and to totally believe that when I confessed You to be my Lord and Savior that I was cleansed of all unrighteousness past, present, and future. When Jesus said on the cross, 'It is finished,' He meant that the full price for the sin of man had been paid. There is nothing more I can do to cleanse me of my sin than to accept You into my heart and believe in the price You paid for my sin. Thank You for shedding Your life's blood for me. From this point forward, I will never doubt again. Amen."

Chapter 7:
Remove Your Mountain
of Depression

Back in the 1970s, the television show *Hee Haw* had a little tune that said, "Gloom, despair, and agony on me. Deep dark depression, excessive misery. If it weren't for bad luck, I'd have no luck at all. Gloom, despair, and agony on me." No one likes depression; in fact, everyone hates it. But it still comes in almost everyone's life once in a while. Even a Christian can have bouts of depression and despair. Depression is sometimes brought about by a chemical imbalance in the body; other times it comes from stress, lack of sleep, or a tragic event. There are many causes of depression. Those in depression feel like the weight of the world is on their shoulders. They may feel unloved, alone, helpless, and hopeless. Some people view depression as a sin or a mental disorder brought on by sin. You may be one who is going through bouts of depression even as you read this book. Don't feel like you are alone; from Bible times until present, people have endured depression. Depression, left untreated, can lead to serious physical, mental, and emotional problems and even to death.

Psalm 40:2: "He brought me up from a desolate pit, out of the muddy clay, and set my feet on a rock, making my steps secure" (CSV).

Psalm 103:4: "He redeems your life from the pit ..."

Psalm 116:3: "The ropes of death were wrapped around me, and the torments of Sheol overcame me; I encountered trouble and sorrow" (CSV).

Charles Haddon Spurgeon said, "Fits of depression come over the most of us. Usually cheerful as we may be, we must at intervals be cast down. The strong are not always vigorous, the wise not always ready, the brave not always courageous, and the joyous not always happy."

Prayer changes things, even depression. If you feel your life is in a pit and you are experiencing depression, the first thing you need to do is take it to the Lord. He should not be our last resort, but our first. My dad used to tell an illustration of a woman who went to her pastor and told him all the problems she had in her life. He promptly replied, "Lady, it sounds like we need to pray." To which the lady replied in a shriek and loud voice, "O, has it come to that?" Listen to what some of the writers of the Psalms did to remedy their depression: "I waited patiently for the Lord, and He turned to me and heard my cry for help. He brought me up from a desolate pit, out of the muddy clay, and set my feet on a rock, making my steps secure. He put a new song in my mouth, a hymn of praise to our God. Many will see and fear, and put their trust in the Lord" (Psalm 40:1–3 CSV). In this passage, the Psalmist gives us two things he did to conquer his depression. First, he cried out to the Lord to help him; and second, he waited patiently for the Lord to respond. Answered prayer does not always come immediately. Sometimes the Lord answers over a period of time.

Psalm 103:3–5: "He forgives all your sin; He heals all your diseases. He redeems your life from the pit. He crowns you with faithful love and compassion. He satisfies you with goodness, your youth is renewed like the eagle" (CSV). In this passage, the Psalmist reminds us where our healing comes from. God is the only one who can speak "Peace, be still" to our soul and our depression.

Psalm 116:1–6: "I love the Lord because He has heard my appeal for mercy. Because He has turned His ear to me, I will call out to Him, as long as I live. The ropes of death were wrapped around me, and the torments of Sheol overcame me; I encountered trouble and sorrow. Then I called on the name of the Lord; 'Lord, save me!' The Lord is gracious and righteous; Our God is compassionate. The Lord guards the inexperienced; I was helpless and He saved me" (CSV). The Psalmist here stated his reason for loving the Lord. The Lord heard him. I have good news for you: the Lord loves you and He will listen to you. When you pray for God to remove your mountain of depression, appeal to His mercy and loving kindness and He will do it. I remember a time when I was driving back and forth from my church field to Oklahoma Baptist University when I had become very depressed. I was burnt out from schoolwork, pastoring the church, family responsibilities, and work. I needed to be reminded that I was not alone and that I didn't have to carry the world's problems alone. I cried out to the Lord to come down and put His arms around me and remind me of His love. He answered my prayer immediately and I felt His presence in the car with me. His love enveloped me and gave me the security I was looking for.

Depression is sometimes unavoidable; it creeps into our lives silently, unexpectedly, and uninvited. If you are experiencing depression, first, don't feel guilty. Don't beat yourself up because you are depressed. Understand that almost everyone experiences depression at some point in his life. Depression is most often temporal; it may only last for a little while. Second, if you are experiencing depression, take action. Take it to the Lord. Open your curtains and let the sun shine in. Open the curtains of your heart and let the Son shine in. Listen to praise music and sing along. Make a list of every good gift you have received from your heavenly Father, such as life, health, family, friends, church, etc. Third, study, believe, and speak aloud the Word of God. II Timothy 1:7: "For God has not given us a spirit of fear, but of power and of love and of sound mind" (KJV).

II Timothy 2:1: "You, therefore, my child, be strong in the grace that is in Christ Jesus" (CSV).

Philippians 2:5: "Let this mind be in you which was also in Christ Jesus" (KJV).

Philippians 4:7–8: "And the peace of God, which passeth all understanding, shall keep your hearts and minds through Christ Jesus. Finally, brethren, whatsoever things are honest, whatsoever things are just, whatsoever things are pure, whatsoever things are lovely, whatsoever things are of good report; If there be any virtue, and if there be any praise, think on these things" (KJV).

And my personal favorite, Romans 12:1–2: "I beseech you therefore brethren by the mercies of God, that ye present your bodies a living sacrifice, holy, acceptable unto God, which is your reasonable service, And be not conformed to this world; but be ye transformed by the *renewing of your mind,* that ye may prove what is that good, and acceptable, and perfect, will of God" (KJV emphasis mine).

If after you have sought the Lord and His Word, you are still experiencing depression, see your doctor and see if there is a chemical imbalance going on in your body. Or see a professional Christian counselor and ask him/her to help you conquer the depression.

REMOVE YOUR MOUNTAIN OF DEPRESSION

Question 1. Do you feel like your life is in a pit? _____

Question 2. Do you want to stay in bed and pull the covers over your head? _____

Question 3. Do you find yourself feeling tired and lethargic doing the most trivial of things? _____

Question 4. Is it more comforting to you to be alone in a dark room with the curtains closed? _____

Question 5. Do you find yourself eating when you are not hungry? _____

Question 6. Are your problems weighing you down and are you spending all your time worrying about them? _____

Question 7. Are you deferring your problems to drugs or alcohol? _____

Question 8. Are you tired and irritable for no reason? _____

Question 9. Are you quick tempered? _____

Question 10. Do you ever have thoughts of suicide? _____

If you have answered yes to more than one of these questions, then more than likely you are experiencing depression. If you are depressed, go back and read the verses in this chapter. Meditate on these verses. Ask God to help you to overcome your depression. Ask Him to raise you out of the pit and set you on a rock.

Prayer Challenge:

Our Father, who art in heaven, Holy is Your name. You are the God of grace, mercy, and light; please lift me out of the pit of depression. Illumine my life with Your light and love. Reveal to me that I am a person of worth and productivity. Show me how I can serve You with a glad heart. I confess to You that Your Son Jesus is the Christ, and that You loved me so much that You sent Him to die in my place. I accept Your gift of salvation by placing my faith in Your Son, Jesus Christ. Take this darkness from me and I will serve You with the rest of my life. Thank You for hearing my prayer. In Jesus' name, Amen."

(Now stand back and witness your answered prayer and see the salvation of God in your life.)

CHAPTER 8:
REMOVE YOUR MOUNTAIN
OF ANGER

Every emotion you have is God-given. Emotions are as real as the five senses. Your emotions are given to protect, enjoy, preserve, enhance, stimulate, regulate, and rejuvenate your life. A person without emotions is like a zombie—a machine—existing, but without life. Emotions reveal your personality. They are revealed through body language, words, and actions. Emotions kept in check are good for both body and soul. But emotions out of control can lead to terrible consequences. Anger is one of our emotions that can get out of control too quickly. *Anger is good when it is directed by a just cause, to invoke a correct response.* For example, you see an obnoxious person who is running through a store knock an elderly lady's groceries out of her hand and he does not bother to apologize or gather her groceries for her. Anger kindled against the offender is just, and a correct response would be to help the woman gather her groceries and apologize for the ignorance of the inconsiderate offender. Anger out of control would ignore the elderly woman, chase the offender down, and beat the stuffing out of him. We have all lost our temper in the heat of a moment and either said something we wish we could take back or done something that we wish we could reverse. Anger out of control can lead to broken relationships, broken hearts, and even death. Anger is a mountain that is built much too quickly and takes much too long to remove without the Lord's help. The Bible is filled with examples of people who have lost their tempers and acted out of anger. Cain killed his brother Abel out of anger (Genesis 4). Moses was a man of anger; he killed an Egyptian task-master, he threw the Ten Commandments and broke them, and he struck the rock to bring forth water. All these events are recorded in the book of Exodus. Saul tried to kill David in 1 Samuel 18:10–11. Jeremiah lost his anger against Israel and asked God to destroy them in Jeremiah 18:19–23.

Quick-tempered, short-fused individuals generally explode in fits of anger over the most trivial of offenses. The problem is not so much with others as it is with self. Angry people are unhappy people. They are people who have experienced loss of jobs, relationships, income, health, power, prestige, or experienced other failures in life. They may have experienced trauma, rejection, exclusion, bullying, or simply may have been ignored. Angry people most often will take their anger out on those they love the most and want to hurt the least. After the infraction, they feel even worse about themselves than they did before the offense. The cycle of hurt, anger, and abuse continues to grow until either there is a breakthrough or a separation between the individuals involved.

There is an old cliché that I love that says to fail to plan is to plan to fail. Proverbs 15:22 says, "Plans fail when there is no counsel, but with many advisers they succeed" (CSV). Anger is an emotion that, without a plan to conquer it, *will*, not *may*, explode out of control. God has given us wise counsel on how to control our anger. If you have accepted Christ Jesus into your heart, you are not alone to deal with anger. You are not powerless to overcome your anger. John 1:12 tells us, "But as many as received him, to them gave He power to become sons of God, even to them that believe on His name" (KJV).   The Bible also gives us wonderful instruction on how to keep our anger in check. Through God's Word and prayer, you can remove your mountain of anger and develop your plan to control it.

Step One: Admit you have an anger problem.

Step Two: Go back and reread chapter 3: Removing Your Mountain of Weakness and Sin. Ask God to reveal to you your inner weakness, hurt, and pain. Ask him to reveal to you why you are angry. To conquer your anger problem, you have to resolve what causes you to be angry on the inside. It may be that you need to begin by forgiving yourself or forgiving someone who has hurt you in the past.

Step Three: Look to God's Word and see how it teaches us to handle anger.

1. Slow down and calm down.
Proverbs 15:18: "A hot tempered man stirs up conflict, but a man slow to anger calms strife" (CSV).
Ecclesiastes 7:9: "Don't let your spirit rush to be angry for anger abides in the heart of fools" (CSV).

2. Exercise self-discipline.
Psalm 37:8: "Refrain from anger and give up your rage; do not be agitated it can only bring harm" (CSV).
Ephesians 4:26: "Be angry and do not sin. Don't let the sun go down on your anger" (CSV).
Ephesians 4:31: "All bitterness, anger and wrath, insult and slander must be removed from you, along with all wickedness" (CSV).

3. Exercise patience.
Proverbs 16:32: "Patience is better than power, and controlling one's temper, than capturing a city" (CSV).
Proverbs 19:11: "A person's insight gives him patience, and his virtue is to overlook an offense" (CSV).

4.   Exercise kindness in word and action.
Proverbs 15:1: "A gentle answer turns away anger, but a harsh word stirs up wrath" (CSV).
Proverbs 15:28: "The mind of the righteous person thinks before answering, but the mouth of the wicked blurts out evil things" (CSV).
Proverbs 17:27: "The intelligent person restrains his words, and one who keeps a cool head is a man of understanding" (CSV).

Step 4: Take it to the Lord in prayer.

My favorite professor in seminary was Dr. Jimmy Nelson. I took his class on the book of Jeremiah. I'll never forget how he got our attention by saying, "Jeremiah, at times, would defend the people of Israel to God, and at other times, he would get angry and say, 'God, kill them and let me watch.' The good news was that he took his anger to God rather than to the people of Israel." He went on to say, "Men, when you get angry with people, take it to the Lord and let Him deal with them and your spirit. He had to correct Jeremiah's attitude and remind him that He was in control. Men, let God be your defense."

When you get angry, make sure it is for a just cause and that you exercise a proper response. Take your anger to the Lord and let Him deal with your heart. Remember Romans 12:19: "Dearly beloved, avenge not yourselves, but rather give place unto wrath for it is written, Vengeance is mine; I will repay, saith the Lord" (KJV).

There is no greater tool to control anger than prayer. Use it.

REMOVE YOUR MOUNTAIN OF ANGER

Question 1. Are you quick to lose your temper? _____

Question 2. If your answer is yes, have you examined your heart to find out what has caused you to be so angry? _____

I recently preached at a church where a young man came that morning for the first time in several years. He had lost an infant child and he had exerted his anger at everyone he loved, including his family and God. He cursed everyone and showed no compassion for anyone. That morning he broke down and wept openly. He knew he needed to be right with God, but felt too ashamed to come to the Lord. When I counseled him, we got to the bottom of his anger. He felt he had let everyone down in his life, including his child that died. He, in fact, was not angry at anyone but himself. He prayed and asked God to forgive him and he invited Jesus into his heart. That morning he left with a burden lifted, a new lease on life, and more importantly, a new relationship with God.

Question 3. Have you taken your anger to God? Have you told Him that you are angry and why? _____

If you haven't done so, do it now! Don't let your anger destroy you.

Question 4. If you have taken your anger to God have you waited on Him to deal with your anger? _____

Question 5. Are you willing to forgive in order to be forgiven? _____

Prayer Challenge:

"Dear Lord Jesus, if anyone ever had a reason to be angry for unjust pain and affliction it is You, yet from the cross You cried, 'Father forgive them for they know not what they do.' I understand now that You were not only praying for those beneath the cross, but for all who would ever sin against You, me included. Thank You for praying for me. If You could forgive me, I can forgive those who have hurt me. Please help me to control my anger. When I begin to feel sorry for myself, please remind me of Your pain and suffering. Help me to see those who anger me through Your eyes. I know You hate the sin but love the sinner; help me to do the same. I am helpless to do this on my own, please give me the power of Your Holy Spirit to control my temper. I ask this in the precious name of Your Son, Jesus, amen."

CHAPTER 9:
REMOVE YOUR MOUNTAIN
OF TEMPTATION

Along with getting to see Jesus, the apostles, Elijah, Elisha, Moses, Noah, Adam, and all my loved ones who have gone before me, I can't wait to experience a place where there will be no temptation in heaven. One of the greatest struggles we have in life is temptation. It shows up at our doorstep far too often, and sometimes we even invite temptation into our lives. We human beings are creatures of habit and of weakness. Satan is a master at finding our weakness and bombarding us with temptation. The comedian Flip Wilson became famous for saying, "The devil made me do it." The truth is, the devil can tempt you, but he cannot make you do anything. We succumb to temptation because the heart of man is bent on doing evil continually. We are born with a sinful and selfish desire to have it our way. As long as we are in the flesh, we have to deal with this awful and most powerful tool of Satan. That is why the Scripture deals with this very issue in a powerful and dynamic way. The Scripture records for us that Jesus Himself was tempted but never yielded to temptation. He, along with our instruction book, the Bible, shows us how to overcome temptation. We have available the tools and means to overcome, but the choice is ours whether or not we use them.

I love the Lord for emptying Himself of the splendor and glory of heaven, to come to this sinful earth and be born as a man. I love the fact that He was tempted but never yielded to temptation. Three times Jesus dealt with temptation in the wilderness and three times He overcame. Satan attacked Jesus in three different areas of weakness in mankind. He attacked in weakness of the flesh, because Jesus was weak from not eating. He attacked Him through the lust of the eyes by showing him the kingdoms of the world and offering it to Him. He attacked through the pride of life by trying to get Jesus to tempt His Father by throwing himself off the pinnacle of the temple. We are going to examine how Jesus overcame the temptations of the weakness of the flesh, the lust of the eyes, and the pride of life and hopefully we will choose to do likewise.

Jesus was hungry, tired, and weak from going forty days without food. He was vulnerable to temptation because of the weakness of the flesh. Forty days without food tends to do that to you. I have trouble going forty minutes without food. Weakness of the flesh is no laughing matter. The cravings of the body are overwhelming sometimes. When we deal with the weakness of the flesh, we must deal with addictions to food, drugs, and alcohol, as well as emotional addictions such as gambling, sex, pornography, laziness, and selfishness. All the above can be taken to extreme levels in one's life with devastating results. Jesus dealt with the weakness of the flesh directly by quoting Scriptures, and he dealt with it quickly. Luke 4:3 tells us, "The Devil said to Him, 'If you are the Son of God, tell this stone to become bread'" (CSV). Satan attacks mentally before he attacks the flesh. He prepares his victim to weaken his defense. Satan knows that Jesus is the Son of God, but he tried to get Jesus to doubt who He is in relationship to God. Satan wins if he can get Jesus to doubt His authority and divine nature; remember, He is God incarnate. If Jesus succumbs to Satan's temptation to turn the stone into bread, it would show weakness on Jesus' part and unbelief in which He truly is. Isn't it ironic that Satan caused the first Adam to fall with the temptation to *take and eat* that which was forbidden, and here he tries to get the second Adam to fall by using the same temptation to *take and eat* a stone by using His divine power to do so?

Satan attacks us when we are at our lowest ebb; tired, hungry, sick, and emotionally drained. He loves to make us feel like we are alone, helpless, and unloved, and especially unworthy of God's love, grace, and mercy. He wins when we begin to doubt who we are in relationship to God, through His Son, Jesus Christ. Second, he tempts us where we are the weakest and most vulnerable to fall.

Jesus conquered this first temptation by quoting the last part of Deuteronomy 8:3: "… man doth not live by bread only, but by every word that proceedeth out of the mouth of the Lord …" (KJV). Praise the Lord; He did not take and eat at Satan's bidding.

We can overcome any weakness of the flesh, be it a one-time temptation, a habitual temptation, or an addiction of some kind, it does not matter. We need to find Scriptures that deal with our particular weakness, memorize them, and quote them until they become our own. When you pray for deliverance from your temptation, quote your memory verse(s) back to God. Ask Him to help you to be strong in the power of His might and turn away from the temptation. It is not a sin to be tempted, but when we succumb to the temptation, it becomes sin.

You may be thinking, that is easy for you to say, but you don't know how strong my temptations are. Satan, that old accuser, will remind you of every time you have tried to conquer a particular temptation in your life, only to have failed. When you are discouraged and you have failed over and over, start believing in the authority of the Word of God. Believe it, claim it, and practice it. When you were a baby, you fell over and over until you finally learned how to walk. The same is true of our spiritual walk as well. I John 4:4 states that "ye are of God, little children, and have overcome them; because greater is He that is in you, than he that is in the world" (KJV). "I can do all things through Christ which strengtheneth me" (Philippians 4:13 KJV).

The second temptation in the wilderness was through the lust of the eyes. Satan showed Jesus the kingdoms of the earth in a vision and offered them to Him if he would worship him. "Then the devil, taking Him up on a high mountain, showed Him all the kingdoms of the world in a moment of time. And the devil said to Him, 'all this authority I will give you and their glory; for this has been delivered to me, and I give it to whomsoever I wish. Therefore, if you will worship before me, all will be yours" (Luke 4:4–7). The eyes of mankind are said to be the mirror of the soul and the portal to the heart. From first man, Adam, to modern man, our eyes have gotten us into trouble. Adam and Eve saw the forbidden fruit in the garden of Eden, coveted it, took it, ate it, and then hid in the garden. Achan saw the Babylonian garment, two-hundred shekels of silver, a gold bar of fifty shekels weight; he coveted them, took them, and hid them in his tent. King David saw Bathsheba, coveted her, took her, and she became pregnant. He tried to hide his sin by having her husband, Uriah, killed in battle. Through the lust of the eyes, sin always works the same way. It starts between our ears, by way of our eyes. We begin to dwell on that which appeals to us; we covet it, we take it, and then we have to hide it. We see, we covet, we take, and we hide. I would hate to think what would have become of the world had Jesus yielded to the temptation of the lust of the eyes. Jesus gives us a very good example of how to overcome the lust of the eyes. He simply turned his focus from self back to His Father God. "And Jesus answered and said unto him, 'Get thee behind me, Satan: for it is written, Thou shalt worship the Lord thy God, and him only shalt thou serve.'" (Luke 4:8). There are some things He understood about Satan. First, Satan is the father of lies. "Ye are of your father the devil, and the lusts of your father ye will do. He was a murderer from the beginning, and abode not in the truth, because there is no truth in him. When he speaketh a lie, he speaketh of his own: for he is a liar, and the father of it" (John 8:44 KJV). Read once again the lies that he told Jesus: "all this authority and their glory I will give to you." The authority was not his to give; all authority belongs to God, and He is the only one who can give it and take it. In Matthew 28:18 we read, "And Jesus came and spake unto them, saying, 'All authority is given unto me in heaven and in earth'" (KJV). Satan offered Jesus authority he did not possess and what he offered was of this earth only. God gave Jesus authority both of earth and heaven. Satan also offered him their glory, the glory of the kingdoms of the earth; again, he offered something that was not his to give. If he could have given their glory to Jesus, it would have been the glory of man only. Jesus received a greater glory, the Glory of God. Satan also said this authority had been given him and was his to give to whomever he chose; again, that was a lie. My brother, Tim, says of a liar, "If their lips are moving, it's a lie." When Satan offers you the world on a silver platter and promises you the lust of your eyes, don't believe it. Run from it. Do not pass go; do not collect your two hundred dollars. Remember, the devil is the father of lies. "The thief cometh not, but for to steal, and to kill, and to destroy: I am come that they might have life, and that they might have it more abundantly." (John 10:10).

"Be sober, be vigilant; because your adversary the devil, as a roaring lion, walketh about, seeking whom he may devour" (I Peter 5:8). When you are tempted by the lust of the eyes, remind yourself that Satan is a liar, and what he offers you is to take you down, pull you away from a right relation with God, and to destroy you. Sin brings pleasure only for a moment; in the end is death and destruction. Change your focus from self back to God, it is He we need to please, and when we are in the center of His will, we will be happy. The happiness he gives will be everlasting.

The pride of life was the third temptation of Jesus. Satan tempted Jesus to tempt God. He took Jesus to the pinnacle of the temple and tried to get Him to jump off to see if God would truly protect him. If Satan had accomplished this, it would show that Jesus did not truly trust God and doubted His word. It would also show that Jesus had so much pride in himself to think God would not allow Him to be hurt if he did something as foolish as jumping off the pinnacle of the temple. Jesus responded by quoting the Word: "It is said, Thou shalt not temp the Lord thy God" (Luke 4:12b KJV). Many times today Satan tries to get us to do something foolish as if God will not permit anything to happen to us. Don't be fooled into believing his lies. If Jesus found it necessary to quote the Scripture, how much more should we, who are weak and so easily duped?

Paul gives us a means by which we may arm ourselves against the deceiver in Ephesians 6:10–18.

"10. Finally, my brethren, be strong in the Lord, and in the power of his might.

11. Put on the whole armor of God, that ye may be able to stand against the wiles of the devil.

12. For we wrestle not against flesh and blood, but against principalities, against powers, against the rulers of the darkness of this world, against spiritual wickedness in high places.

13. Wherefore take unto you the whole armor of God, that ye may be able to withstand in the evil day, and having done all, to stand;

14. Stand therefore, having your loins girt about with truth, and having on the breastplate of righteousness;

15. And your feet shod with the preparation of the gospel of peace;

16. Above all, taking the shield of faith, wherewith ye shall be able to quench all the fiery darts of the wicked.

17. And take the helmet of salvation, and the sword of the Spirit, which is the word of God;

18. Praying always with all prayer and supplication in the Spirit, and watching thereunto with all perseverance and supplication for all saints."

In verse 10, Paul told us to be strong in the Lord and the power of His might. Oh, how true that Scripture is. It is impossible to defend ourselves against the devil except by the power of the Lord. The only way you can have the power of the Lord is by receiving Him into your heart. "But to as many as received Him to them gave He power to become sons of God" (John 1:12). Those who have received the Lord into their hearts are the ones who have the power to stand against the wiles of the devil. Living the Christian life is impossible without Christ and the power of the Holy Spirit in your life. If we are going to overcome temptation, we have to do it in the power of His might.

Next, Paul tells us to put on the whole armor of God so that we can stand against the wiles of the devil. He then begins to describe the armor. The first piece of armor Paul describes is the belt of truth in verse 14. The belt of truth is what gives us the strength to stand. Have you ever seen a weightlifter with a wide belt around his waist? He uses the belt to strengthen his back while lifting. A person of faith first comes to the Lord when he recognizes truth. Jesus said He was the way, the truth, and the life in John 14:6. You will never be able to stand against the lies of the devil until you know the truth of Jesus Christ. No wonder Paul begins with that piece of armor.

The second piece of armor that Paul describes is the breastplate of righteousness. Truth reveals Jesus to us and the breastplate of righteousness covers our sinful heart. What God sees when He views the Christian's life is the righteousness of His beloved Son, Jesus Christ. The breastplate of righteousness is the opposite of what the devil has to offer, which is evil. Paul once again pictures the right piece of armor. How could we possibly protect our hearts without the righteousness of Jesus covering it? The third pieces of armor are the shoes of the gospel of peace. Shoes are made for walking; we are to be on the move with the gospel of peace. We sometimes advance, sometimes hold our ground, and sometimes retreat. Whichever direction the gospel takes us, we take peace with us. Having the shoes of the gospel of peace is the opposite of what the devil wants us to experience, which is torment and chaos.

The fourth piece of the armor is the shield of faith. In ancient days, a warrior would protect himself with a shield. The shield pictured here is a Roman shield, which was a long, curved rectangle shield. It protected the whole body of the one carrying it. When the Roman army was shot with their enemy's arrows, they would overlap their shields above their bodies and the arrows would hit the shields. They soaked their shields before going into battle so that if the enemy shot flaming arrows at them, the shield would extinguish the flame. We take the shield of faith to quench the fiery darts or arrows of the devil. I like this description of the devil's arrows. Without faith, we would be burned by the devil's lies and temptations. Sin always jumps up and bites you when you least expect it. It burns the soul and spirit of man. We must take the shield of faith.

The next piece of armor Paul describes is the helmet of salvation. A helmet is to protect the head, and specifically, the brain. Think about why Paul describes the helmet of salvation as that which protects our heads. Sin always begins between our ears in our brains. We see with our eyes, we covet with our hearts, we take or do that which we know is wrong, and then we hide. If we wear the helmet of salvation, it protects our eyes, our ears, our tongues, and our brains. When we accept Jesus into our hearts, we are covered from head to toe with Jesus. We take up the armor of God and wear Him proudly and triumphantly.

Finally, Paul tells us we have a weapon we can use. The weapon is the sword, which is the Word of God. Our weapon to use against the temptations of the devil is the Word of God, just as Jesus used the Word to defeat the devil in the wilderness. Now you can stand against temptation because you are armed with the armor of God and you have at your disposal the strongest weapon known to man, the Word of God.

I can't close this chapter without giving you one more important verse to beat temptation with. "There hath no temptation taken you but such as is common to man: but God is faithful, who will not suffer you to be tempted above that ye are able; but will with the temptation also make a way to escape, that ye may be able to bear it" (I Corinthians 10:13). Words cannot express how valuable this verse has been to me over the years. It reminds me that there is a way to conquer our temptation. Here is this verse in my own words: "There is no temptation that you have ever experienced or will experience that others have not already experienced. You are not alone in your temptation. God is faithful to be with you through every temptation, great or small, and He will not permit you to be tempted beyond your ability to endure it. With every temptation you experience, He will show you a door of escape so that you will be able to overcome it." Our job is to recognize the door of escape and take it. The door of escape will be different in every temptation, but the first place to look for the door of escape is in the Holy Scriptures.

You know where you have been tempted in the past, so find those verses that deal with your past temptations, recognize them as doors of escape, and memorize them. Look for the obvious doors of escape which may include just saying no, walking away, or staying away from the source of your temptation. All through my ministry, I have dealt with people who have had an addiction to something or someone that they have escaped from, or have been delivered from, only to go back to surround themselves with the same thing or same people that brought them the temptation to begin with. Not only will God show you a way to escape your temptation, He will also show you doors that you should not enter to begin with. Use your brain, listen to the heart of God, and chose the correct doors for your life.

REMOVE YOUR MOUNTAIN OF TEMPTATION

Question 1. Where is your area of weakness?
Circle one:

A. Weakness of the Flesh (addictions, gluttony, no self-control, etc.)

B. Lust of the Eyes (pornography, covetousness, selfish desires, etc.)

C. Pride of Life (thinking too highly of self, haughtiness, pride, gossip, putting others down, etc.)

Question 2. How often does Satan attack you with temptation in your weakest area? Circle one:

A. Hourly B. Daily C. Weekly D. Monthly E. Yearly

Question 3. Do you place yourself in harm's way to be tempted?
Circle one: A. Yes B. No

Question 4. When you are tempted, do you look for a way of escape?
Circle one: A. Yes B. No

Question 5. What are ways you can avoid placing yourself in harm's way of temptation?

_____

_____

_____

_____

Question 6. What Scripture references have you found that deal with your temptation? Make a list below:

_____

_____

_____

_____

_____

Question 7. Will you work at memorizing your Scripture references by at least one per week?
Circle one: A. Yes B. No

Question 8. Do you have an accountability partner?
Circle one: A. Yes B. No
If your answer is no, find someone who will stand in the gap with you and ask them to be your accountability partner.

Question 9. Do you have a plan of action to help you overcome your temptations?
Circle one: A. Yes B. No
If your answer is yes, write out your plan of action.

_____

_____

_____

If your answer is no, make a plan of action.

Question 10. Have you put on the Armor of God today?
Circle one: A. Yes B. No

Prayer Challenge:
"Dear Lord Jesus, thank You for emptying Yourself and becoming a man so that You could identify with us. Help me to learn from the way You dealt with temptation in Your life and do the same in mine. Help me to avoid placing myself in temptation's way.

Give me the inner strength to be self-disciplined. Help me put on the armor of God. I am now putting on the belt of truth. Lord, I know You are the way, the truth, and the life. I will stand strong in truth and keep it ever before me. Now, Lord, I am putting on the breastplate of righteousness, not my righteousness, but Yours. By placing the breastplate of righteousness over my heart, I know it will be protected from the attack of Satan. Help me study Your life and find those areas in Scripture that show me your righteousness so that I may emulate Your life in mine. I am now putting on the shoes of the gospel of peace. I will stand, move forward, or retreat in these shoes so that I may lead others to You, dear Lord. Now, Lord, I am picking up the shield of faith in which to protect myself from the fiery darts of the devil. I will march with this shield, advance with this shield, do battle using this shield, and overcome using this shield. Now, Lord, I am putting on the helmet of salvation, which will protect my brain, my thoughts, my eyes, my ears, and my tongue. I am now picking up the only weapon You have given us to use and that is the sword of the Spirit, which is the Word of God. I will memorize all the Scripture that I can, use it all I can, share it all I can, and defeat Satan with it. I will continually pray and seek Your face, asking for strength to overcome all my temptations. Lastly Lord, show me a way of escape in the midst of my temptations and I will take it. I love You, Lord, and I praise you for loving me. In the precious name of Jesus I pray, amen."

CHAPTER 10:
REMOVE YOUR MOUNTAIN
OF ADVERSITY

When I began this book, I planned to have it finished by December of 2009. Little did I know, I would lose December 2009 through February 2010. By the time you finish reading this chapter, you will understand what I am talking about. Overcoming or removing your mountain of adversity is something my wife and I are very familiar with.

Adversity can be defined as misfortune, adverse happening, hardship, difficulty, danger, harsh conditions, and hard times. Everyone faces adversity in their lives at some time or another, but overcoming it is a whole different story. In this chapter you will learn how we overcame our adversity and how you can overcome yours.

Our adversity began September 30, 2008, when my dad passed away. My dad had been a pastor and evangelist for fifty-six years. In 1998, he was diagnosed with Alzheimer's. At first, we did not want to admit that Dad had the disease, but time proved us wrong. My youngest brother told me he was angry at God and he couldn't understand why God would permit something like this to happen to a man who had given his whole life to the gospel ministry. I told him that God had a reason and that we were just at a point in our lives where we could show the world what kind of men Dad had raised. We could either mope and be mad about it, or we could embrace Dad and help him through his illness with as much dignity as possible.

I was on a mission trip to Utah the week before Dad died. I had prayed that God would allow him to live until we got home, and that is just what God did for us. We got home on Saturday, Dad went into the hospital on Sunday, and died at four o'clock Wednesday morning. I got to hold his hand and sing his favorite hymns to him the last four hours of his life. I will never forget those last hours, and when Dad took his last breath, I told him to go to Jesus. What most people saw as an adversity was really a blessing. Many times we perceive adversity when we should be seeing God do His handiwork. What Satan meant for evil, God meant for good.

April 11, 2009, was the day before Easter, and it was a beautiful day in Oklahoma. We had just gotten our new horse on which Glenda was so seriously hurt, as you have already read. Once again, our adversity was turned to triumph because of our relationship with God. I remember the feeling I had when God showed up in my spirit. He overwhelmed me with His love and presence. I knew that whichever direction the accident would take, God was with me. Once again, God showed up and what Satan meant for evil, God meant for good.

No one could believe my mother would outlive my dad because she had congestive heart failure, kidney failure, and was on dialysis three days a week. She was in the nursing home and pretty much bedridden. She longed for the day God would call her home. Just after Glenda's accident, Mother told me she wanted to go home to heaven. I told her that I needed her to help me through Glenda's accident. She said that was all she needed to hear and she wanted to stay. Mother lived long enough to see her 82nd birthday on July 19, 2009. It was a wonderful day with all of her boys with her. We had cake and ice cream, which she dearly loved. August 27, 2009, Mother took her last breath. Once again, I was able to be with her, and she got her wish of going home to Jesus. What Satan meant for evil, God meant for good.

Time passed and Glenda healed from her accident. We were looking forward to Thanksgiving, but Glenda's mother got sick and went into the hospital. On the Friday after Thanksgiving, she had a brain bleed and died the next morning. She had M.S. for forty years and she, too, had been praying for God to take her home. Glenda, her dad, our daughter, Jeanie, and her mother's sister, Dot, were with her when she died. I did her graveside service in Enid, Oklahoma, on Friday. I told everyone that day that Jesus was going to come back soon, and I promised that he would come in their lifetime. He was either going to come back for His Bride, the church, or He was going to come back for us individually. What Satan meant for evil, God meant for good.

Little did I know that a week later my life would change forever. My youngest son, Rodger, had taken vacation time for the week after Glenda's mother died and he and I had planned a hunting trip to Woodward, Oklahoma, for that following week. Even though Glenda's mother had died, Glenda insisted that we still go on our hunting trip. So we left from Enid that day and went to Woodward. We had a great time hunting on the Van Valley Farms, nineteen miles north of Woodward. On the day we left, we said our goodbyes to Dwight and Peggy VanDorn and headed home. Thirty miles west of Enid, Rodger and I had a great conversation. I told him to promise me that he would stay in church and raise his children up to know and serve the Lord. I also told him to tell his brother, David, and his sisters, Jeanie and Nette, to do the same. Just after I told him that, a man in a pickup truck flew out of the ditch a hundred yards in front of us. The man driving the truck turned right into our headlights and was trying to hit us head on. Rodger swerved into his lane to keep from being hit, and the man in the pickup went off the road on our side, turned back into us, and hit us from the passenger side where I was sitting. When I saw the lights coming at me, my thought was, am I going to live or die? The next thing I remember is Rodger crying into his cell phone and telling his wife that I was dead. I raised my head and told him I wasn't dead and to calm down. The whole side of my van was wiped out, and my door was crushed in on me. Rodger jumped up on his seat and leaned over and put his arm around me and asked me where I was hurt. I told him that I was hurt in the front, the back, and my sides. I could feel the bones moving in my back. Just about that time, a man came up to our van and told us he had already called for help and the ambulance was on the way. When the ambulance arrived, an EMT came to my door and said, "Mr. Keim, I heard you preach in my church (First Baptist Church of Fairview, Oklahoma)." He told me he was going to have to cut the door off to get me out. After the door was off, he said they were going to get me out and it was going to hurt. I told him to go for it and just as he started to get me out, I screamed for them to wait. I took a big breath and told them, "Now," and they pulled me out on a board. The pain was excruciating. They took me to Enid's Bass Memorial Hospital. There they did x-rays and stabilized me. My family got the news of my accident and came to the hospital in Enid. Before they got there, they had to put a chest tube in my right side because my right lung had been punctured by a broken rib. Overall, I had broken two vertebrae in my neck, three vertebrae in my lower back, all my ribs on the right side, half the ribs on my left side, my collar bone, and my sternum. My kidneys and liver were badly bruised and I was in very critical condition. When Glenda got the news of our accident, she prayed and told God she could not do another Friday night like the one she had had the week before where she lost her mother. She told God, "This time you are going to have to carry me." She said it was like God came down and picked her up and held her. She knew that I was going to live from that moment on. What Satan meant for evil, God meant for good.

Glenda and our friends, Dr. Robin and Ruth Stevenson, arrived at the hospital where they learned of my condition. Robin told me later that he did not believe I would make it because he had seen so many soldiers die in Viet Nam who sustained injuries like mine. He told me every one of them died. That night, I knew I was in a critical condition and that I could possibly die. I asked Glenda, "What in the world are we going to do?" I knew the only income we had was from the revivals that I preached and the support from our monthly contributors. I knew that if I lived, it would be a long time before I could preach again. Our monthly contributions had dropped off due to the economy, and there would be no revival income. She told me that God would take care of us. She had already trusted God to take care of all our needs. Now, five months after the accident, I can tell you that God has taken care of us in a miraculous way. What Satan meant for evil, God meant for good.

The doctors at Bass Hospital in Enid called for a life flight to take me to Oklahoma City, but my daughter, Jeanie, told them that I needed to be in Tulsa where most of our family lives. They agreed to take me to St. John's Hospital in Tulsa. We later learned that St. John's is the best trauma hospital in Oklahoma. I believe that had I been taken anywhere else I would have died. As they were loading me onto the helicopter, Glenda told me I was finally getting my wish to fly on a helicopter. I had always wanted to ride on one but had never had the opportunity. This wasn't my idea of the kind of trip I had in mind. I remember flying to Tulsa, getting out of the helicopter, and finally, my family arriving back in Tulsa. After further examination, the doctors told Glenda that they were going to put me into an induced coma. They told her I would never survive the pain. They also told her that I would be in the hospital for several weeks. None of us knew that I would be in a coma for nearly two months.

For the next seven weeks, it was a daily struggle to keep me alive. Doctors and nurses would work around the clock to keep me going. One doctor told Glenda he had never seen a man as broken up as me walk out of the hospital alive. At one point, he told her that out of all the patients they had in ICU, I was the most critical. That weekend, five of the patients around me died. God kept me going. Many preachers, friends, and relatives came by to visit me. They were all taken aback when they came into my ICU room and saw my body swollen to over four hundred pounds. At one time, I had thirteen tubes going into my body. They kept pumping fluids into my body to keep my organs moist, flexible, and functioning. One of the most interesting things about my ICU experience was the room they put me in. The doctors and nurses call it the miracle room. Up until that time, no one had ever died in that room. They thought I was going to be the first. One of my doctors was a Christian man who was frank with Glenda about my condition, but also very compassionate. He told her that there were going to be some good days and also some bad days. He was right, but every time there was a bad day, God sent someone to visit who ministered to my wife. What an awesome God we serve.

I hope you are beginning to see God showing up for us at the right time with the right person. He was always in control of the situation: first, the witness to the accident who called for help, the EMT who had heard me preach, my daughter convincing them to send me to Tulsa, St. John's Hospital placing me in the miracle room, and having a Christian doctor take care of me. What Satan meant for evil God meant for good.

The inevitable happened: I got pneumonia. The doctors told Glenda that my lungs had turned hard like wood and that they would not expand. They told her that they believed the pneumonia would take my life. News spread fast and far as people around the world began to pray for me. One pastor told me he had a missionary friend in Africa who he had emailed so much about my condition that the missionary told him that it was like he knew me personally. The doctor called my family in for a meeting. He told them that if he thought I had a brain injury that he would pull the plug on me that day, but because my brain was still functioning, he said he would continue to fight for as long as it took. He told Glenda that he didn't have time to talk to the family much so if they didn't see him, that was a good sign, but if they saw him coming, it meant something else was going wrong. The very next morning he came walking up to Glenda and she told him she did not want to see him. He told her I had taken a turn for the worse and that there was only one more thing they could do to save my life: put a tube on the left side of my chest. She told him to do it and then got back on the phone and told everyone to start praying. The pastor of First Baptist Church of Tahlequah, Buddy Hunt, came to visit that day, and as he was exiting my room, he heard two nurses talking. One said, "Mr. Keim won't be here two more days." He said he called back two days later and they told him I was still alive and fighting for my life. He called back a week later and the nurse said that I was actually getting better. What Satan meant for evil, God meant for good.

I woke up in late January from my coma and a nurse asked me if I knew the date. I told her I believed it was the end of November or the beginning of December, and she told me that I had been in a coma for the past several weeks and that it was January 27. It dawned on me several days later that I had missed Christmas, three of my children's birthdays, New Year's, and so much more. Glenda asked me if I saw Jesus, and I told her I did. She then asked if I had seen my parents and her mother and I told her I did. Then I told her Jesus said there were many souls to save. I don't remember that experience now, but Glenda said I was adamant about it. Others asked me if I was aware of what was going on around me during my coma, and I told them that I wasn't, but that my brain was very active during my coma. I experienced many things during that time that defy imagination. I experienced going back to several places I had lived as a child. I experienced dreams or visions that were so real to me that I believed I was living them. Some were wonderful and good, others were very frightening. One of the things I remember believing was that I was being held a hostage and that I had my hands bound. I thought I was being kept alive so my body parts could be harvested and sold. I thought to myself that I was a strong man, and that if I tried real hard, I could break the bonds. Glenda told me that my hands were bound because I kept trying to pull all the lines out of my body. She said I was pulling on the restraints with all my strength.

The greatest thing I remember experiencing while in my coma was walking with Jesus. He was in a dark tan wool garment that went all the way to the ground. I looked down and I had on the same wool garment. I was amazed at what Jesus looked like. He was my height, six feet tall, with an olive complexion, and the one thing that I thought was curious was that his beard was very low on his cheeks and his cheeks above his beard were very smooth with no stubble. I have always wondered how we would know it is Jesus when we see Him since we have not seen Him in the flesh. When Jesus showed up while I was in a coma, He didn't have to introduce Himself to me; I just knew immediately it was Him. I was afraid to say anything to Jesus and I wanted Him to speak first, so I just walked and stayed quiet. Another thing that I thought was interesting was that we were walking in the light of Christ. Everywhere we walked we were in light, but there was no light shining down on us. Outside of the light was total darkness. As we were walking, the apostle Paul showed up on my right side. He began to talk to me and I guess I showed some pride and arrogance that Paul had showed up to talk to me. Jesus spoke for the first time and said, "No, Charlie, that is the wrong spirit." I turned back around and Paul was gone. Now I was positive I wasn't going to say anything until given permission or asked a question. All of a sudden, Moses showed up on my right side, Jesus still on my left. Can you imagine being between Jesus and Moses? I was so moved with humility walking with Jesus and Moses that I felt absolutely broken between them. Jesus turned and looked at me with the most beautiful smile and said, "Charlie, that is the right spirit." That was the end of my vision. I remember looking at Jesus thinking, I am an artist; I have to remember His face so I can paint it. When I came out of my coma, I couldn't remember His face from His nose up, but I could remember from

His nose down. I still can see His cheeks and His beautiful smile. After getting out of the hospital on February 19, Glenda and I drove to North Carolina in April to attend a chalk art school. We stopped in Nashville to spend the night, and in our motel room, we watched the History Channel about *The True Face of Jesus* taken from the Shroud of Turin. Scientists have found a way to make a 3-D image of the body and face of the person whose image is on the shroud. When they showed His face, I began to cry. Glenda asked me why I was crying and I told her that the image they were showing was the very image I saw in my vision. The only thing they had wrong was that his beard was not as high on his cheeks as they made it out to be. Through the good and the bad that I experienced while in my coma, there is one thing I know for sure: what Satan meant for evil, God meant for good. I would go through all the pain, the entire trauma, and my brush with death to see Jesus again.

By now, I hope you have picked up on the theme of this chapter: that what Satan meant for evil, God meant for good. As believers, we can bank on Romans 8:28, which says, "And we know that all things work together for good to them who love the Lord and are called according to His purpose." Notice what this verse is not saying. It is not saying that everything we experience is good or pleasant to go through, but out of every situation something good can come. Souls can come to Christ as the result of a testimony of someone who has experienced certain events in his life. A person who has experienced trauma, loss, or other tragedies can share how Jesus brought him through. Overcoming adversity demands that we take a look at the Scripture and seek God's face through prayer to help us cope and conquer our trial.

The first step in conquering our adversity is to accept the event or trauma as part of God's permissive will. You cannot change what has already been done. How you react to it makes all the difference not only in the world, but in eternity. Souls will either be turned away from God because of your negative acceptance or they will be turned to God because of your Christian strength.

The world responds to tragedy with critical eyes; they see only the bad. Job said it this way in Job 2:10, "But he said unto her, Thou speakest as one of the foolish women speaketh. What? Shall we receive good at the hand of God, and shall we not receive evil? (adversity) in all this Job did not sin with his lips" (KJV emphasis mine). A believer looks beyond the bad and looks for God to show up. II Corinthians 5:7 says, "For we walk by faith, not by sight" (KJV).

The second step in overcoming your adversity is to call out to God immediately after the event or trauma takes place. Seek His face. King David gave a wonderful insight on how to do this in I Chronicles 16:11: "Seek the Lord and His strength, seek His face continually." Jesus tells us in Matthew 7:7–8, "Ask, and it will be given to you; seek, and you will find; knock, and it will be opened to you; For every one that asks receives; and he who seeks finds; and to him that knocks it will be opened."

The third step is to remember past times when God showed up in your life, resolved a problem, met a need, or worked a miracle and testify to others what was done. King David said in I Chronicles 16: 8–12, "Oh, give thanks to the Lord! Call upon His name; *Make known His deeds among the peoples!* Sing to Him, sing psalms to Him; Talk of all His wondrous works! Glory in His holy name; Let the hearts of those rejoice who seek the Lord! Seek the Lord and His strength; Seek His face evermore! *Remember His marvelous works which He has done, His wonders, and the judgments of His mouth"* (emphasis mine).

The fourth step is to remember to give thanks in all things. "In everything give thanks for this is the will of God in Christ Jesus concerning you" (I Thessalonians 5:17 KJV). Listen, when I saw Glenda on the ground I was not thinking of giving thanks for her accident. I was concerned whether or not she was going to live. In the midst of the tragedy, God showed up and I had immediate peace. My heart was thankful for the presence of the Lord. In my accident, when I heard the EMT say that he had heard me preach, I was thankful that God reminded me He was present. Throughout my ministry, I have had individuals ask me how they could give thanks for a particular tragedy in their life. God is not asking you to be insensitive to an event in your life nor is He asking you to say something or do something crazy that is out of touch with reality. The truth is, when we experience something tragic, we grieve, we are in shock, we sometimes get angry at others or even God. God understands our frustration, our hurt, and our pain, yet He wants us to praise Him for who He is, what He is capable of doing in the midst of our situation. Thank Him for not abandoning or forsaking us. In your greatest adversity is when you are going to need God the most in your life. Don't wait until the tragedy happens before you learn to praise Him. By building a wonderful relationship with God now, you will be better equipped to beseech Him when you need Him the most.

The fifth step is to *trust God* to get you through your ordeal. Trust in the midst of the trial, just as Glenda trusted God to bring me back. When the doctors gave her no hope, she still trusted God. Trust Him even when things don't go the way you expected them to go or wanted them to go. There is one thing you can always count on and that is that God always keeps His word. He has promised you that He would not leave you nor forsake you. Hebrews 13:5c tells us, "For He hath said, I will never leave thee, nor forsake thee." We may not understand why we are going through our trauma, loss, and pain. We may never know the answer this side of heaven. Yet God has revealed to us that He knows what He is doing. "For as the heavens are higher than the earth, so are my ways higher than your ways, and my thoughts than your thoughts" (Isaiah 55:9 KJV). Proverbs 3:5–6 says, "Trust in the Lord with all thine heart; and lean not unto thine own understanding. In all thy ways acknowledge Him, and He shall direct thy paths" (KJV). The mountains of adversity we face are huge, many times overwhelming, yet God is always strong. He is never taken by surprise; He knew before you faced your trial what you would face and how you would handle it. He is waiting on you to seek Him. He loves you so much that He has already sent His Son, Jesus Christ, to die for your sins. Jesus is waiting for you to cast your burdens on Him, for He cares for you. "Casting all your care upon Him; for He careth for you" (I Peter 5:7). What are you waiting for? Trust the One who can do something about it.

REMOVE YOUR MOUNTAIN
OF ADVERSITY

Question 1. What is the biggest adversity you have ever faced before in your life? Did God show up in your trial?

_____

_____

_____

_____

_____

Question 2. How did you react to your adversity?

_____

_____

_____

_____

Question 3. How did God show Himself strong in your trial?

_____

_____

_____

_____

Question 4. What lessons of life did you learn through your adversity?

_____

_____

_____

_____

Question 5. Have you ever told anyone who is going through a similar tragedy how God ministered to you?

_____
_____
_____
_____
_____

Question 6. Have you been able to look back on your life and see the handiwork of God?

_____
_____
_____
_____
_____

Question 7. Would others be drawn closer to God or away from God by your response to your trial? Explain.

_____
_____
_____
_____
_____

Question 8. What part of your trial are you having the hardest time trusting God with? Explain.

_____
_____
_____
_____
_____

Question 9. Have you forgiven the one who has hurt you or yours?

_____

_____

_____

_____

_____

Question 10. Have you forgiven yourself for an adversity that you may have caused? Explain

_____

_____

_____

_____

_____

Prayer Challenge:
"Oh God, my Father, Your thoughts and ways are above mine. Many things in this life I cannot understand. You have helped me through past ordeals and You have always been faithful to be there for me when I needed You the most. Yet even now it is so easy to take my eyes off of You and, like Peter, to begin to sink in the sea of life. Help me in my weakness, in my lack of faith and trust. Help me to become a person of great faith and trust in You regardless of my circumstances. I will always love You for who You are and what You have already done for me. Thank You for Your grace and mercy. Thank You for the peace that You can bring not only now, but always. Thank You for your Son, Jesus Christ, who can speak to the wind and the waves, "Peace, be still." I need You, Lord, now and forever. Remind me, Lord, of past events in my life where You showed up and helped, even those times I am not aware of. Help me to seek You early, before the event takes place in my life. Help me to be proactive in preparation for whatever may take place in the future. I love You, Lord, and thank You in advance for whatever may lie ahead for me. In the precious name of Jesus, Your Son, amen."

PHOTO GALLERY

My van and the truck that hit us

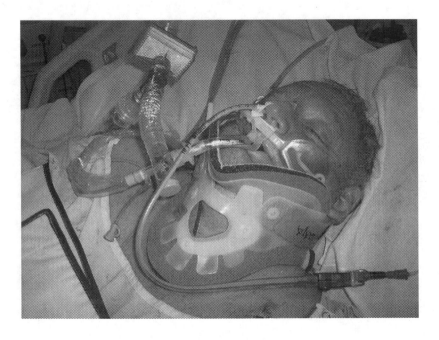

This photo was taken shortly after I was put into an induced coma. Over the next seven weeks, doctors and nurses would fight to keep me alive, along with thousands of prayers on my behalf.

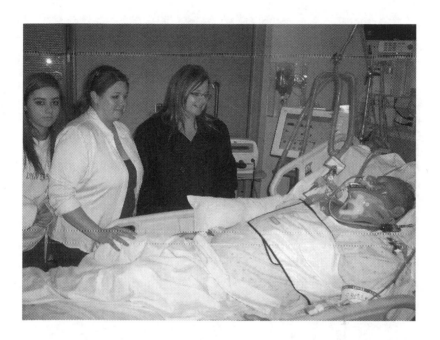

A special thanks goes to my dearest friends, Ed and Shirley Dowty's four daughters, Beverly, Becky, Amanda and Beth who stayed by my side throughout my stay in the hospital. Amanda and Becky were there almost every day. In the picture above, Beverly is on the right, Amanda in the middle, and Beverly's daughter, Shelby, on the left.

Charles F. Keim

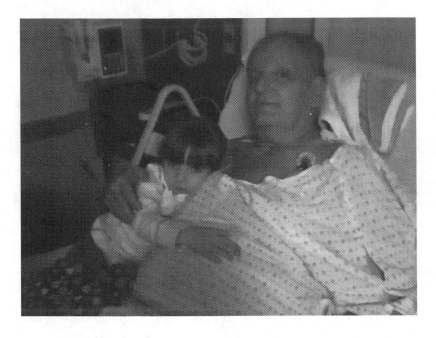

*This photo is of me with my only grand-daughter, Lillie
Grace Keim, at St. John's Hospital in Tulsa, OK.*

This photo is of me and Glenda while I was in rehab. Glenda is the epitome of the Proverbs 31 virtuous woman. Words will never be enough to say how grateful I am for her, her faith, love, and devotion to God. Her faith never wavered that I would live, and she has taken very good care of me both in the hospital and out. Thank you, Glenda, for forty years of wonderful marriage. I will always love you.

This picture is of me and little Emma. She did not know me other than as Mrs. Jeanie's dad. She told her mother to be quiet in their car because she was going to pray for me and it would take a while.

This photo of my family was taken February 14, 2010, at Riverview Baptist Church. I had a one-day pass from the hospital. I was still in a wheelchair at this time. What a blessed man I am to have such a wonderful Christian family. Present in the front row are, from left to right: Nette, Malachi, Elijah, me with Mason on my lap, Sam, Glenda, and Sawyer. Back row is Matt McSherry, my son-in-law, my daughter, Jeanie McSherry, my son, David, with his son, Dawson, his wife, Amy, their son, Larami, Luke, and my son, Rodger, is in the very back. Rodger's wife, Diane, was not there that day since their children were sick at home. This has been a very trying time for all of us, but praise the Lord, He brought us through. Healing is still going on, both physically in me and emotionally in all of us. I don't know how people cope with their tragedies without the Lord.

It is my earnest prayer that all who read this book will be able to live a fuller, more productive and victorious Christian life. Too often we are quick to drop new believers to fend for themselves in their quest for discipleship. Just as a baby needs nurturing, so does a new babe in Christ. When one accepts Jesus into his heart, he has been born again. II Corinthians 5:17 says, "Therefore if any man be in Christ, he is a new creature; old things are passed away; behold, all things are become new" (KJV). New believers, as well as other believers, are shocked to find out that they are subject to the same fragilities of man. We still have our emotions and lives to deal with. With this book of guided Scriptures and prayers, I hope the believer will find it easier to cope in life; not just to cope, but to live a victorious Christian life.

My prayer for you:
"Oh, Father, Master, Designer, and Sustainer of life, I pray for all who read this book. Take my feeble effort and by the power of the Holy Spirit, touch their lives. Help them to not only read the Scriptures recorded in this book, memorize them, and use them, but to search the Bible for more truth for what they are going through. May it be an inspiration to all. Thank You, Father, for showing Yourself strong in my and my family's lives. What we have been through is worth it all if lives will be changed and challenged by our testimonies. Thank You, God, in the precious name of your Son, Jesus Christ. Amen."

This book is dedicated to the memory of my parents, Clarence (Buddy) and Maxine Keim, who loved me and my brothers and raised us in a godly environment. Dad taught us the Word of God from the time we were born. They set a great example of living the Christian life three hundred and sixty-five days a year. They were consistent in their faith, love, and devotion to God and their family. This book is also dedicated to my mother-in-law, Joan Ashcraft, and our special adopted mom, Momma Betty Appelton. All the above went home to be with the Lord between September 30, 2008, and March 2, 2010. They all were a wonderful influence in my life. They taught me much about faith, love, and devotion, and they will be missed and remembered until we have our reunion in heaven.